...and the pursuit of healthcare....

considering challenges with Dr. E.A. Stead, Jr.

by

Robert L. Bloomfield, M.D., M.S.

Clinical Assistant Professor, Department of Medicine
Bowman Gray School of Medicine,
Wake Forest University and
Director, Evergreen Health Promotion
Winston-Salem, North Carolina

edited by Carolyn F. Pedley, M.D.
Assistant Professor, Dept. of Med.
BGSM, Wake Forest Univ. Physicians
and Arthur Finn, M.D.
Professor of Medicine and Physiology
UNC-Chapel Hill, NC

Harbinger Medical Press
Box 17201
Winston-Salem, N.C. 27116
(336) 768 9827 or (336) 659 6250
or fax-(336) 659 6239

Library of Congress Catalogue Number: 00-193051

ISBN: 0-9612242-1-5

*...and the pursuit
of healthcare...*

FS Heart Failure

***...and the pursuit of
healthcare....***

considering challenges with Dr. E.A. Stead, Jr.

FG Forgetting   by

Robert L. Bloomfield, M.D., M.S.
with comments from Drs.
Michael DeBakey
Henry D. McIntosh
John Laszlo and
Arthur Finn

Foreword by J. Willis Hurst, M.D.
Addition by Bernard Lown, M.D.

Dedication:

To Drs. Soma Weiss, Frank Engel, John Hickam,
James Warren, Jack Myers and many others that carry
on a special tradition that we respect and to all those
students who re-inspect their studies.
**and in memory of Dr. S. T. Bloomfield, Dartmouth '34, M.D., Dart. '36,
BU, '40, Boston City Hospital, '43**

and to Adam and Laura
who may carry on absolutely any tradition they wish to.

Acknowledgements

Special thanks to Drs. J. Willis Hurst, Michael DeBakey, and
sister, Lois, Bernard Lown, Henry McIntosh, John Laszlo, and
Arthur Finn for their kind contributions, Drs. Pedley and Agwu
for their proofreading, Drs. G. Wagner and G. 'Mack' Bryan for
their input and Ms. Evelyn Stead for her feedback.

Table of Contents

Also available from Harbinger Medical Press:
   Mnemonics, Rhetoric and Poetics for Medics
      volume 1
      volume 2
      volume 3
      volume 4
         [all different]
   Cardiovascular Mnemonics
   Pocket Mnemonics
   Physician, Humor Thyself
   Hypertension Handbook
         [for patients and practitioners]
   Hypertension Textbook
   Practicing the Art While Mastering the Science....
      By Bernard Lown, M.D. [NOBEL PRIZE RECIPIENT]
   Orthostatic Hypotension
      By Red Herring [song on cd + poster]
         [#1 OF SERIES]

*free catalogue available or call or write for information
and details*

...and the pursuit of healthcare....

considering challenges with Dr. E.A. Stead, Jr.

by

Robert L. Bloomfield, M.D., M.S.

Special Thanks to:
Mr. David Pounds, laidback, layout artistic director
Dr. Carolyn Pedley, main editorial advisor
Ms. Lou Chickadaunce, artist out of residence, outa town
Mr. Adam Samuel, southeastern scholar, philosophical consult
Ms. Laura Simone, cool footnoter and header work
Mr. John Standish, multimedia engineer, cheap advisor
Mr. Glain Schneider, chief cheap advisor and Beantown resident
Mr Tom Clark, paramusical consultant, former Yellow Cabette
Ms. Catherine Miller, PA-C, Wake Forest U., P.A. Program
Mr. Al Kelly and Mr. John Cibelli, printing consultants
Drs. Galen Wagner, Bernard Lown and J. Willis Hurst
Drs. McIntosh, Finn, Laszlo, and [of course] the patient Dr. Stead

Editor's Note

"...[my] intention...is to shorten long-winded discourse and synthesize the various ideas....not to neglect the advice [of my mentors]...." [21]
-Ian Botlan, *'THE PHYSICIAN',* fifteenth century

The years have given Dr. Stead time to reflect and reassess his career and therein lies one of the purposes of this book. I, myself, think back to the spirit with which I entered this privileged profession that gave me a unique perspective. I can still recall the altered ideals of students and young practitioners I've taught, who have pursued the discipline of medicine.

Nothing has seemed more effective for fortifying forgotten personal promises in students, doctors, N.P.s, and PAs than gaining an understanding of the history of medical practice. The life and times of Dr. E.A. Stead, Jr. is only one highlight; but a bright one. The interested reader is directed to the writings of Avicenna and Locke, both physicians, among other philosophers, on the study of sciences. More recent are the writings of Karl Popper. John Dewey's pragmatism has a special relationship to the present work.

The 'empiricists', like Locke and Hume, championed experiential knowledge gained through the five senses. My own experiences with patients, practitioners and students have emphasized the need for a sixth sense, as well, in practice; 'common sense'; that's a sense that Dr. Stead championed. I won't even touch upon another sense that defies definition; 'intuition' or its closely allied characteristic, 'judgement'.

I wrote this volume with the input of Dr. Stead and others in the hope of inspiring others to continue the pursuit of helping patients in ways that remain immeasurable. May these words deepen one's dedication to health sciences and reinitiate readers into the circle of devotion for the nonmaterial rewards of studying and practicing Medicine.

R.L.B.

PREFACE
by RLB

*Many clues to the unknowns in medicine are locked in the library, waiting for someone to open the right book at the right time.   [22]
Alphonse Raymond Dochez*

*Physicians, like beer, are best when they are old.   [22]
Thomas Fuller*

abnormis saiens crassaque Minerva
[for translations of Latin phrases, see end of each section and penultimate page]

A person's accomplishments speak more forcefully than any curriculum vitae [C.V.]. Many great physicians have C.V.s which contain reams of paper that constitute enough cellulose to be considered a high fiber diet or fill an extra volume of Encyclopedia Brittanica. These printed accolades accompany prestigious practitioners when they leave their home bases and travel to lecture at some distant institution of higher learning.

1

Dr. Stead has always tended to minimize the size of his C.V., not just to save trees and preserve plant-life, but because he felt that it might not fairly represent him, and it really didn't make much difference in the long run or the big scheme of things. [I've actually altered his C.V., for this book, especially the post-Duke portion]. Also, he didn't intend to leave Durham, NC to talk at some other institution's grand rounds that frequently; he'd rather have been at the hospital late at night with the medical housestaff, students and patients. And whom did he wish to impress elsewhere, anyway? Teachers of medicine, clinicians and administrators of medical centers don't have all that much reason or time to publish research articles; and Dr. Stead eschewed adding his name to papers for which he didn't actually do basic hands-on work. So, one may not find his name attached to all the work he stimulated. But, the effects he had on disease concepts, the approach to the patient and medical education have been pervasive and long-lasting. 'Long-lasting', by the **Stead** definition of the term, denotes a greater time span than is customarily referred to in nonbiologic circles. His Darwinian perspective of 'geological time' encompasses the ice age, the Jurassic era, as well as the geriatric era, all of which tend to eclipse fame, fortunes [or four chins] and the like.

Ask anyone who presides over a medical center, chairs a Department of Medicine or directs a medical, physician's assistant, or nursing school and they'll all acknowledge the impact that 'Stead'-like practice has today; some 35-45 years since the peak of his career. He left an imprint in the sand. His

2

power has been carried on and developed by his medical descendants and proponents in the form of his mode of housestaff training, his bedside teaching methods, his educational approach, etc. All these things appear to have more lasting power than the names on any ephemeral, 'breakthrough' journal paper.

Dr. Stead has had personal lasting power too. He's in his 90's, is extremely vital and has few regrets from his past history. No doubt, he's had some time to think about medicine from a healthy distance. In terms of medical history, many agree that Sir William Osler had the greatest impact upon American Medicine for the first half of the twentieth century; the latter half belongs to a brilliant thinker born in Georgia, Dr. Eugene Stead. Anybody who was anybody in medicine past 1945 knew Dr. Stead and, in turn, he knew everybody that was anybody. A rich who's who in medicine can be garnered best from other books listed in the reference section at the end of this book, and from Dr. John Laszlo's unpublished manuscript-*The Doctor's Doctor [28]*. What is also clear in those previous treatises and explained in this volume is that Dr. Stead was at the forefront of a fundamental change in medical education, practice and research. He was a phenomenon that considered medicine a formidable challenge and an enjoyable lifetime endeavor.

The present book was written, in contrast to prior publications, to describe Dr. Stead's approach and his philosophy. These distilled concepts are some of his greatest gifts to our profession; concepts which may be lost in the recounting of Dr. Stead's eventful career. Yet, much of his wisdom can be applied to many aspects of our lives; this wisdom may be key in our difficult pursuit of healthcare for all.

Please excuse my occasional asides which may transgress on a hallowed, serious subject. They were meant for my own tragicomic relief and should not be misconstrued as any disrespect. I, too, realize the immensity of Dr. Stead's accomplishments. Although his C.V. is included below, this abridged list and the short summary this volume covers in the chapters that follow, do not do the man justice.

Translation of Latin phrase: An unorthodox sage of rough genius.

Introduction [and unscientific abstract]
by RLB

The bedside is always the true center of medical teaching.
[22]   Oliver Wendell Holmes

tecum habita noris quam sit tibi curta supellex

A book of this multifaceted nature [biography and documentary mixed with philosophy, poetry, and, at times, a stream-of-consciousness or unconsciousness, and, rarely, stream-of-stupor] deserves something akin to a scientific abstract in order to make the approach to this subject somewhat familiar to our readership. However, unlike what one's accustomed to at the end of many journal articles, the epilogue to this volume will not reiterate the phrase: "... further research will be required to support our findings." Rebuttals, on the other hand, will gladly be accepted and forwarded to me by the publisher. Readers should know that Dr. Stead has reviewed these pages and has been offered the opportunity to refute these summaries or support their veracity; he's been known to change his mind, usually for good reason. Writing this volume has been difficult and has kept me awake at night. However, if the reader would allow me to borrow some

5

words of Dr. Stead's, "...; I know *that,* now tell me something I don't already know."

A foreword is presented by Dr. J. Willis Hurst, a long-time friend of Dr. Stead. The foreword has been moved more forward than its usual position. This is preceded by a shorter preface and an introduction. An editor's note precedes all of these and gives me room to express my own impressions, spanning a much shorter acquaintance time than Dr. Hurst.

Chapter one describes Dr. Stead's early cardiovascular interests, including his clarification of the 'opening snap' of mitral stenosis [a heart valve disorder], his mentor's interest in orthostatic hypotension, his work and concepts regarding heart failure [CHF]. It also covers his experiences at Emory with pericardial tamponade, shock, the development of his cardiac catheterization laboratory, renovascular physiology, etc.

Chapter two covers a basic, but circuitous, timeline of Dr. Stead's development, especially his time at Harvard and Peter Bent Brigham Hospital and contains an explanation of a previous biographical note by his colleague and friend, Dr. Paul Beeson. It also briefly notes the careers of Drs. Walter Kempner, Grace Kerby and some others.

Chapter three clarifies the first two chapters by explaining briefly some of the better-known of Dr. Stead's relationships with his medical mentors, colleagues and students. It also touches upon some of his basic philosophical tenets.

Chapter four is a reconstruction of a post-retirement time when Dr. Stead spent several months assisting in the restructuring of Baylor Medical School. It contains a description of this process with a short note by Dr. Michael DeBakey and others who have ties to Baylor Medical School.

Chapter five is entitled 'The Mind of Medicine', and describes Dr. Stead's philosophy on the roles of psychiatry/psychology in the care of patients, as well as in the presentation of the patient's chief complaint. An explanation of Dr. Stead's concepts of patient subgrouping, the structure of the nervous system, and the use of computers is briefly presented.

Chapter six covers primarily the post-Duke years; years of semi-retirement and retirement. This was a time for reflection and describes some concepts not explored in earlier chapters; in particular, a philosophy of teaching. A poetic interlude is included in this chapter.

Chapter seven is a recapitulation with annotations of Dr. Stead's C.V. with additional quotes credited to him. Interspersed in references from the C. V. are some other quotes and a correspondence from Dr. Stead.

Chapter eight contains excerpts from two addresses by Sir William Osler, apropos to this presentation. A historical note has been added.

Chapter nine is an adaptation from the Archives of Internal Medicine describing physicians of the past and future, written by Dr. Stead for a symposium honoring his friend and colleague, Dr. John Hickam. Further discussions of his philosophy are pursued.

Chapter ten consists of comments about Dr. Stead by several colleagues and former medical house officers [They've also had time to think].

Chapter eleven is a commentary by an admirer and friend of Dr. Stead's, Dr. Bernard Lown, on the role of medical education and access to healthcare in less developed nations and in less endowed segments of the U.S. population.

A closing epilogue followed by an afterthought, poetic interludes and a list of references concludes the book.

These last pages also list the English translations of the Latin phrases that introduce various sections along with an offering of an adaptation of an older well-known poem apropos to the preceding text.

Translation of Latin phrase: Realize how much you have still to learn.

Considering Challenges with Dr. Stead

FOREWORD by J. WILLIS HURST, M.D.

Knowledge is not a looseleaf notebook of facts. Above all it is a responsibility for the integrity of what we are, primarily of what we are as ethical creatures. The personal commitment of a man to his skill, the intellectual commitment and the emotional equipment working together as one, has made the ascent of man. [22]
William Blake

I never studied under Eugene Anson Stead, Jr., but I have studied his words and actions.

Why did I study Stead? Here is the story. I first heard Gene Stead when he "debated" Eugene Landis, who was Harvard's well known physiologist, at a medical meeting in Boston in 1948. At that time I was a cardiology fellow with Dr. Paul White at the Massachusetts General Hospital. Whereas most lectures and discussions are promptly forgotten by listeners, I can still hear Stead talking in his unique, sagacious, and dramatic way to emphasize that physiological information could be used to understand patients with constrictive pericarditis. I was greatly impressed when Stead accepted a point made by Landis that Stead had not previously considered. I recognized Stead was searching for the truth. At that point in time, I did not foresee the relationship I would have with Gene Stead in the years that followed.

Stead, was born in Decatur, Georgia, which is adjacent to Atlanta, on October 6, 1908. He had a relatively lonely childhood, but read incessantly and claims he was afraid of girls. He went to Emory College on a scholarship and borrowed the money from the Rotary Club to go to medical school. He entered Emory medical school on a bet made with Robert Bayley [who later became known for his work in electrocardiography], during a chess game, that he could make an A in anatomy even though one-third of the class failed. He made an A in anatomy and many other subjects as well. He, without knowing it, became increasingly interested in how people learn. He asked himself questions about everything he did and sought the answers himself. He read medical books other than those assigned to him. He decided that attending lectures on subjects that were better discussed in books was a waste of time. He would read in textbooks what the lectures said in a few minutes and would cut classes. He would then make A's on the exams. Actually, his medical degree was temporarily withheld because a professor complained that he did not attend his classes, although he made an A on the exam. Top officials saved the day and overruled the professor. During this period he also became aware of the fact that studying every day was not much better than cramming before an examination because either method of preparing for the examination would work, but, he discovered unless the information was used repeatedly in a thought process after the examination, it would be forgotten. So, he concluded during these formative years that going to lectures is not the most efficient way to learn and that cramming for examinations was acceptable. The 'forgetting curve', even for the student who studied each day was operative unless the information was actually used. He enjoyed pursuing the answers to questions he had about patients and attending ward rounds with J. Edgar Paullin, an Osler trained clinician. Paullin served as a volunteer Chairman of the Department of Medicine at Emory.

Stead joined the medical house staff at Peter Bent Brigham Hospital in Boston in 1932 when Henry Christian was chief of medicine. He later became a surgical intern for one year, but decided he was too clumsy to be a surgeon. He confessed to being so clumsy that "he could not walk through a door without hitting one side of the doorframe." He also concluded that he liked to work on people who were awake rather than sleeping under the influence of an anesthetic. Stead then became Chief Resident in Medicine at the Cincinnati General Hospital where Dr. Blankenhorn was Chief of Medicine. It was there he learned how to organize a medical service that would attract excellent medical residents and where everyone taught. Even then he was recognized as a teacher and was referred to as 'professor'. Soma Weiss visited Cincinnati General Hospital and while there offered Stead a position at the Thorndike Laboratory in Boston. Stead eventually accepted his offer and simultaneously acted as Chief Resident in Medicine at Boston City Hospital. He held both jobs in order to make $1800 a year. At that time he was paying part of the Emory medical school tuition for his brother, William Stead. Soma Weiss became Stead's role model. Soma Weiss seemed to know everything that was written about disease, but would learn even more about the problem by meticulously studying the patient with the disease. Stead emulated that method of learning and refined the question-asking system to challenge himself and others. He and those around him asked questions about patients and pursued the answers. Stead worked in the laboratory and was interested in edema and how mercurial diuretics worked. He claims, however, that he was not technically adept in the research laboratory and that he did more thinking than "working". He became the creative thinker behind many important scientific studies and administrative moves.

Soma Weiss became Chief of Medicine at the Brigham. Stead moved with him to the Brigham and he, along with several other bright faculty members, created an excellent medical service where important research was also performed. Stead was becoming internationally known and at the age of 33 was offered the Chairmanship of Medicine at Emory University in Atlanta where he had graduated. Soma Weiss advised him to accept saying, "Go where you are needed" and "It is time for you to find out whether you can move from being a man of promise to a man of achievement." Soma Weiss died of a ruptured aneurysm of the brain in 1942, before Dr. Stead moved to Atlanta. At that juncture, Stead was better suited for the 'rough and tumble' medicine of the South. He had already accepted the offer to become Emory University's first full-time Professor and

Chairman of the Department of Medicine. Stead did act as Chief at the Brigham until he left for Emory in 1942 and George Thorne, a very accomplished physician, became Chief at the Brigham.

When Stead arrived at Emory in 1942 he found no other full-time teachers and there was no clinical research. At that point, the first two years of Emory Medical School were attended on the Emory campus and the clinical years were attended at Grady Memorial Hospital. Stead arrived to take charge of the medical service at Grady, but found that Emory officials had not informed the volunteer Chief of Medicine that Stead had been appointed Chairman of the Department and would also be the Chief of Medicine at Grady. Stead thought, "I will be here every day and many nights, but the volunteer Chief only comes a few hours a week." The students and house staff would soon view him as Chief because "I will run the service." He lived by the rule: 'Authority is not given, it has to be taken.' In addition, he thought, "If in one year I am not viewed as being in charge, I will enter practice." At the end of the year everyone, even Dr. Paullin, knew he was the Chief and offered to give him a party. He declined, saying he was too busy to attend parties.

Academic medicine at Emory took a giant step forward as Stead became the Pied Piper, recruiting brilliant people to work in Emory's Grady Hospital. As an example of Stead's drawing power, some friends from the Brigham: James Warren, Abner Golden, John Hickam, and Ed Miller announced they planned to arrive at Grady on July 1, 1942. Stead responded, "I don't have any money." They responded, "We will be there--We did not ask you for permission; We just thought you ought to know about our plan." Stead used house staff and fellow money to pay them. Stead, whose salary was $8,000 a year, recruited Paul Beeson to join the Department of Medicine for $4,000 a year. With the encouragement and help of Alfred Blalock, Stead decided to develop a cardiac catheterization laboratory at Grady. There were only two other cardiac catheterization laboratories in the world at the time. One was in London and one was at Bellevue Hospital in New York. Jim Warren went to Bellevue and learned the technique from Cournand. He returned to Grady to study patients with shock. This was needed because World War II was raging and shock was a common problem in our troops. Accordingly, Stead organized his team to study shock. The team worked night and day. When they were not studying shock they studied heart failure. They also placed the cardiac catheter in many places that had not been considered for physiologic exploration. They studied the kidney, the liver, etc. These physiologic studies were published and read throughout the world. James Warren reasoned that if one pushed the cardiac catheter into the right side of the heart, there should be an increase of oxygen in the right atrium in patients with atrial septal defect. He demonstrated the truth of this in Dr. Stead's catheterization lab. This was the first diagnostic catheterization ever performed. The study was published in 1945 in *The American Journal of Medical Sciences.* Stead was the thinker behind many of the reports that were published, but he never added his name to a paper unless he personally participated

14

in the work. The classic description of "Fluid Dynamics in Chronic Heart Failure" by Warren and Stead in *The Archives of Internal Medicine* in 1944, remains a benchmark in medicine and should be read by anyone interested in the evolution of physiologic knowledge of heart failure.

Stead recruited Paul Beeson, Phil Bondy, Jack Myers, and others to join the Department of Medicine. Later, many of the members of the Department of Medicine became Department Chairmen at other medical schools. The administrative forces at Emory insisted that Stead become Dean of the Medical School as well as Chairman of the Department of Medicine. He reluctantly did so. He knew how to be a dean, but it interfered with time he wanted to spend on the wards--trying out ideas in the laboratory---and teaching---and teaching---and teaching.

He was offered and accepted Chair of the Department of Medicine at Duke in 1945. He wanted to develop a private service for housestaff and students and return to the activity he loved. There all could learn as they assisted attending physicians in the care of the patients. Duke already had a private outpatient clinic; within the same hospital, and a private and public service waiting to be developed. Although he loved Emory, he moved to Duke, where he developed a renowned Department of Medicine.

His Pied Piper activity never ceased. At last count he had trained about 37 department chairpersons and academic officers, as well as an untold number of division directors. Therefore, as he gave up the chairmanship at Duke at age 60, his influence was still felt in many medical schools. This is his legacy; it is not likely anyone will accomplish more.

During his tenure as Chairman at Duke he changed the medical school curriculum and in 1965 established the first Physician Assistant Program in the country. I started such a program at Emory two years later and wrote him about it. He replied, "Imitation is the finest form of flattery."

After he gave up the Chairmanship at age 60, he spent a year at Cornell in order to be out of the new Chairperson's way. Jim Wyngaarden followed Stead as Chair at Duke and continued the excellence he inherited. In New York, Stead continued to think of ways to improve and make ward rounds. He returned to Duke as Distinguished Professor at the Veterans Hospital and worked in a nursing home in order to learn more about geriatrics and about many aspects of caring for the aging population. He continued to make teaching ward rounds at Duke until the age of 86.

Early in his career at Duke, he and Evelyn, his wife, and their three children built a home on Kerr Lake, North Carolina. They built almost all of it with their own hands. This is where Gene Stead and Evelyn currently live and think. As discussed subsequently, you can't stop his creative thinking. Kerr Lake is kind of like his perpetual 'Walden Pond', though it is larger-a reservoir for ruminating.

Let me explain why I studied Stead. When Stead left Emory for Duke in 1946, Paul Beeson became Chairman of that Department of Medicine in Atlanta. I joined Beeson to work with

Bruce Logue in cardiology in 1950. Beeson became Chairman of Medicine at Yale in 1952, and was replaced at Emory by Eugene Ferris, but Ferris then became Director of the American Heart Association. I was offered his position at Emory University School of Medicine in the fall of 1956. The legacy of excellence left by Gene Stead and Paul Beeson had always permeated the environment at Emory so, seeking the advice of two wise men, I spent the night at Gene's home in Durham and Paul's home in New Haven. Gene told me, as Soma Weiss had told him, "Go where you are needed. It is time you determine if you are a man of promise or a man of achievement." Beeson offered me encouragement and support. They are both great men as well as great doctors.

The expansive halls of Grady Hospital were filled with stories of Gene Stead and Paul Beeson. I've talked with Stead on the phone. I read everything he wrote and watched his administrative moves. I invited him to Emory in 1982 to discuss the creation of a Division of Geriatrics. We have talked frequently on the phone. He continues to teach me. It was during the last visit that I was able to interview him.

Gene Stead taught me many things, but his insight and discussions about how people learn was his greatest contribution to me. I have made a mighty effort to "pass it on" to students, house officers, fellows, and colleagues. He has always emphasized that *information* is the first step in the thinking process. But *thinking* is more than that--it is the rearrangement of facts (information) into a new perception. *Learning* is achieved by the repetition of the process.

He pointed out that lectures are not the most efficient way to learn. He emphasized that the value of a lecture depended on what the listener did with the information after he or she left the lecture room. He pointed out that reading without purpose is not as good as asking a question and pursuing the answer. As Jim Warren noted, he was always in a "search mode", always asking questions; and not a "sponge mode"; sopping up facts.

I learned from Stead that the key to developing a productive faculty and exciting house staff program was to recruit the best young people and set the highest standard. They could excel in teaching, patient care, or research. The emphasis at any institution is always influenced by the available facilities, the budget, and administrative structure. Gene Stead downplays his role in developing a number of department chairmen. He claims that they were all self-motivated, bright people and did not need his help. He is, however, unabashedly proud of his efforts to create the Physician Assistant Program, because the activity was started de novo.

During the last few years Gene has dreamed of the creation of a book that contained basic biologic facts. He assigned me a specific chapter and he would write the chapter on proteins. He has encouraged me to start a new medical school with only 24 faculty to counter the schools who claim they have 1,000 faculty. Following my publication of a book on 'The Heart' 'for children', written with my grandson, he urged me to develop a whole set of books on biology that would appeal to kids.

All of the above thinking took place when Stead was approaching 90 years of age. His creative juices are still flowing. This is why former faculty members gather at his home on Kerr Lake. This is why physician assistants visit him often. He is still the pied piper of people who are fascinated by the words he utters because they signify a creative mind in action.

Some people say a lot, but have little impact on others. Eugene A. Stead talks and writes far less than others, but his words and sentences have a profound influence. Why is this true? First of all, Stead is a creative thinker. He sees the world as being different from the way others see it. He sifts and recognizes a lot of information to create what seems to be a simple statement. The statement is often shocking, but is at the same time an intellectual achievement. For example, his definition of a teaching hospital is, "a hospital where everybody teaches" or "what this patient needs is a doctor." In those words he reveals his wisdom. The first aphorism implies that trainees teach faculty and each other as well as faculty teaching trainees. The second aphorism emphasizes that knowing about disease is not the same as "taking care" of patients with disease.

Several books and articles have been written about Stead and this will not be the last one. Dr. Robert Bloomfield and various contributors should be congratulated for providing insight into his creative thinking and his contribution to Medicine.

Sources of information in order of publication date.

Warren JV, Stead EA. Fluid dynamics in chronic congestive heart failure. Arch Intern Med. 1944;73:138.

Brannon ES, Weens HS, Warren JV. Atrial Septal Defect: Study of hemodynamics by the technique of right heart catheterization. Am J Med Sci. 1945; 210:480-491.

Hurst JW. The quest for excellence: The history of the Department of Medicine at Emory University School of Medicine 1834-1986. Atlanta: Scholars Press. 1997.

Hurst JW. Eugene Anson Stead, Jr., M.D. A Conversation with J. Willis Hurst, M.D., Am J Cardiol. 1999; 84:701-725.

J. Willis Hurst, M.D.
Consultant to the Division of Cardiology, Emory University School of Medicine; Former Professor and Chairman Department of Medicine 1957-1986, Emory University School of Medicine Atlanta, GA

1

The Opening Move: **The Opening Snap and Other Cardiovascular Questions**

by Robert L. Bloomfield

I don't like work- no man ever does-but I like what is in the work-the chance to find yourself. Your own reality-for yourself, not others-what no other man can ever know. [22]   Joseph Conrad

Davus sum, non Oedipus

Much has been written and said about Dr. Eugene Stead. His career development would require volumes. The present abbreviated rendition has to be a partial treatment of a complex subject. Dr. Stead followed some of the rules, and bent others, adopted from the refined medical establishment. The medical world, however, was not fully prepared for the unorthodox assault on Medicine that would result from the odyssey of Eugene Stead.

It was 1940 in New England. The war overseas was being viewed from afar and the mood at the Peter Bent Brigham Hospital was guarded. There was a sense that improved orderliness and greater efficiency needed further attention at the hospital. Down south, the boll weevil had devastated farmland, and people were still reeling from the effects of the Great Depression. Dr. Stead

21

worked alongside his chief and mentor, Dr. Soma Weiss, for about $4000 per year. Dr. Weiss's secretary, Evelyn, and Dr. Stead were seeing each other, later to be married at Dr. Weiss's home.

Now, the compulsiveness and thoroughness of Dr. Stead required that every patient that was admitted to the medical service had to be questioned and examined by Eugene Stead himself; he personally saw and reviewed every case. Every patient had a story to tell and, sometimes, a physical finding which distinguished him or her from others.

Eugene Stead was an unusual mixture-domineering when it concerned clinical matters, but timid in social situations. Those kinds of situations arose frequently in Bostonian life. He had gained some culture from his time in Cincinnati; Gilbert and Sullivan operas, books like Beard's, *"American Civilization"*, and a variety of cheeses ripening on the Midwestern windowsills. Yet, he remained more at home inside the hospital. In the hospital, there were medical findings still being named after devoted physicians. Discoveries were being made; not so much by the newer technology, as by the meticulous observations and pathological correlations, often at autopsy.

When Dr. Stead found something that he had not been taught or that was clinically unfamiliar, he did what a good physician has always done and should do: he would admit his lack of knowledge [though, few do this readily], ask his mentor for leads, and do more reading and examining to rout out the answer to his question. Dr. Weiss would have to admit that this characteristic along with his devotion to the work ethic, made Dr. Stead a formidable clinician. This process of meticulous problem-solving had occurred on several occasions when auscultating the heart. The cardiac portion of the physical examination was one of the most challenging segments of the patient work-up; one which required knowledge of physiology, as well as anatomy and pathology. A sense of rhythm didn't hurt either along with a willingness for repetition and close attention--the ability to focus in spite of distractions. Since his youth in Georgia, he was very able to learn, shutting out the clamor of his busy family members and proceeding with his reading or studies. He had been brought up in a family that valued education and learning; the concert piano they purchased on their limited income attested to that.

His sense of rhythm had always been acute, as long he was not asked to sing a third-part harmony. He was not that proficient at carrying a tune, though musical murmurs were not a major challenge. According to his colleagues in Boston, he always stayed busy; he was not just whistling Dixie. His clinical acumen gained from years down south was a source of envy to the less-experienced housestaff at Harvard. Back in medical school days at Emory he had lived at Grady Hospital. He readily accepted extended service and was always readily available to deliver babies. He did more deliveries than most obstetricians and also readily covered for the pediatric interns when they were on vacation. Stead was very comfortable with a plethora of patients with any difficulty, cardiac or non-cardiac.

As technology has advanced to determine different aspects of cardiac physiology and anatomy, the cardiac part of the physical examination has become more abbreviated and certain therapeutic themes have become apparent. In that bygone era, however, Dr. Sam Levine walked these halls and Dr. Paul White's multivolumed textbook on heart disease was an essential reference. Yet, the 'opening snap' of mitral stenosis, a heart valve disorder arising from previous rheumatic fever, had not been well-appreciated by doctors. Its relation to other cardiopulmonary findings, like lung rales-a finding of fluid overload from a diseased left side of the heart-had not been well worked out. When a clinical finding is not well-delineated among a constellation of symptoms and signs, it can not be used to subclassify disorders, subgroup patients, form prognostic or diagnostic information, or to be applied to a particular case for patient management. These are practical considerations which rely heavily on an end-product: a physician's final judgement. This end-product was the most valuable asset that the patients were seeking from the experienced, learned physician; an asset that they found even in the youthful Dr. Stead.

Dr. Stead always listened carefully to his patients during the history and physical. Auscultating the chest, he sometimes heard a distinct sound following the closure of the aortic and pulmonic valves [S2]. He questioned Dr. Weiss, reviewed the literature, and processed information from the patient, as well as from the autopsy table. He deduced that this extra sound emanated from a thickened, but somewhat flexible mitral valve, damaged by the body's response to prior rheumatic fever.

This 'opening snap' of mitral stenosis is heard accompanying a rumbling murmur at the apex [the bottom of the main chambers] of the heart's projected position on the patient's chest. Though it is a subtle sound, some maneuvers that the physician puts the patient through, make it more audible: laying the patient on the left side, making the patient exercise, cough, and execute the Valsalva maneuver-attempting to expire against resistance [like forcing air against a closed airway]. Therefore, the observation of the opening snap and the associated murmur was a complex process involving listening, reading, and history retaking; an intimate interaction for the patient, as well as for the doctor. There was a good reason to obtain this knowledge: not to outdo the other physicians and residents on ward rounds, but to assess the severity of the stenosis. So, careful, repetitious listening, maneuvering and observing had a real practical purpose with personal implications. The discovery cannot be useful until it can be applied to help the patient. Dr. Stead made a large portion of his contribution in the form of late-night labor when most people in the busy city were sleeping. In a warmer climate, like sultry Atlanta, one could accomplish more in the cool, wee hours; when mental, medical inspiration might come.

The Ice[pick] Age

Not many of his colleagues suggested that Dr. Stead return to Emory, from which he received his medical degree after his being part of a Harvard-associated hospital in an important medical role. His mentor, Dr. Soma Weiss did, however; he told Dr. Stead that leaving Boston for Atlanta was an opportunity to find out if he could lead the medical school at Emory to prominence; he did. He left 'Beantown' with regrets, for the basic-training battleground and bedpans of the 'bible belt.' It certainly was not that smooth after he arrived. There was a black Grady Hospital and a white Grady Hospital and the actual Emory campus was miles away from both; there were other impediments to learning from private, as well as public patients. The physicians in control of these facilities were not prepared to relinquish their powers and positions. To even broach the subject of desegregating the service was unheard of. Yet, Dr. Stead had helped desegregate the wards in Cincinnati, during his chief residency under Dr. Blackenhorn. In Atlanta, while he wasn't able to join black and white Grady, he treated patients of any color equivalently. And the nurses at the black Grady were pleasantly surprised to see Dr. Stead rounding on their indigent patients so frequently.

Dr. Stead found himself in Atlanta with a position that had not been well-defined; his academic appointment had been misinterpreted by him, since neither medical chief from the two Grady hospitals was willing to give up their directorships. However, he had not come down from Boston unaccompanied. He was a 'medical magnet' and Drs. James Warren, Abner Golden, John Hickam, and Edward Miller demanded to join him down south as he left the northeast. There was no choice on his part. Dr. Stead did not only attract veteran academics, he also attracted younger students of medicine. Even when he was at Harvard, his clinical experience had outstripped his peers and many flocked to him for his medical knowledge. Many sensed the dedication that emanated from him regarding patient care, medical know-how, and teaching.

When Dr. Stead was molding the medical teaching program at Emory, he invoked his academic support from young and older, more experienced students of medicine. He supplemented this support to fortify his position as the Chairman of the Department of Medicine by investing something that other contenders had little of: *time*. Dr. Stead spent much of his time in the hospitals: rounding on patients, teaching at the bedside, and sharing knowledge with colleagues. When he was not on the wards, people knew where to find him: in his makeshift, low, sometimes flooded, non-air-conditioned office [pre-AC] in the basement of the black Grady hospital, downtown. His office was very modest, with small high windows looking out on the parking area of the Coca Cola plant. Many soft drinks were consumed at quasi-equatorial Emory and the university-associated hospitals downtown; after a heavy rain he might be found mopping up the water from the floor; and if you were there, you had better have helped. He wasn't in some other city lecturing about some esoteric subject. The main place he taught was in the hospital; and even then, as he warned his students and house officers: "You can't trust solely the information presented in lectures. You should read books and articles, ask clinicians, ask laboratory personnel, ask deaners [animal/lab. caretakers]; and for heaven's sake, ask the patient again." It would take a perceptive and resourceful practitioner to ask the same question in a novel way to get a patient answer, which would provide new and useful information.

So, his position was fortified, no small thanks to his team that stood behind him, to the support of devoted faculty and students, and to the establishment at Emory that had to concede to his plans for bettering the university. Improvement in the program required financial support. Funding, however, was not easily obtained. The war effort required that any research program had to have a direct relationship to problems experienced by the troops overseas. The population of Atlanta experienced some combative behaviors, but nothing as largescale as was going on overseas.

Late on any Friday night, a houseofficer might look up as he was furiously recording a history and physical from an evening admission and see Dr. Stead sitting next to him, inquiring, "Got anything interesting?" Friday nights were busy times for the Emergency Department, when fights resulted in icepick wounds to the chest. These were unusual trauma cases that would present as a piercing of the underlying cardiac wall, leading to profuse bleeding into the pericardium-the fibrous covering around the heart. They were fertile cases for reversing a potentially lethal cardiac disorder. They were also a fine means for learning and understanding cardiac physiology. Finding "pulsus paradoxicus" among other symptoms and signs would clinch the diagnosis and initiate a surgical or emergency room sequence to relieve the 'choking' on the cardiac output. Since his days at Emory Medical School, Dr. Stead's alma mater had become known as a cardiac trauma center in the U. S. because of these cases. These bloody 'massacres', as the ice pick attacks were called, might occur on Friday, Saturday, or Sunday. Dr. Stead would always be in the hospital on those nights to afford himself the opportunity to see these patients. Atlanta was a center for other medical opportunities, as well. Dr. Stead had several avenues open to his skills.

Soon after Stead came to Atlanta, he brought Dr. Frank Engel and helped fix up a temporary apartment for this member in which his faculty could reside. In that process, the landlord was required to paint the walls. In his rush and artistic frenzy, the housepainter did a quick job and the resident cockroaches were caught dead in their tracks in the yellow baseboard paint. In Atlanta, doctors experienced all kinds of things they might not find in more refined surroundings. There's something to be said for going where one's skills are really needed, too; to boldly go where few doctors have dared to venture before. "Darn it Jim, I'm a doctor [kinda like 'Bones'-who's doing an orthopedic rotation, presently], not merely a subspecialist, Cap'n Kirk!!"

Shock Research, Concepts of Heart Failure and Cardiac Catheterization

The total budget for the medical school when Dr. Stead returned to Atlanta in 1942 was less than $26,000.00. There was certainly room for more funding to carry out the improvements that Dr. Stead had planned. The federal government was committed to the war effort and supported medical research that was related to this. After considering several ideas, studying the response to "shock" was decided upon. This fortuitous decision led to a better understanding of the consequences of another important cardiovascular malady: heart failure; it also helped replete a financial need of the university. Dr. Stead had no notion as to the budgetary requirements of his proposed project. Thanks to a typographical error, a misplaced period, Emory received $50,000.00, not $5,000.00 as first proposed; that higher amount was just enough money to complete the study.

This study, and the lines of thinking it created, led to the conceptual framework that is still employed today in the management of patients with congestive heart failure [CHF]. In shock, the organs were not being perfused because the blood volume was low, usually from bleeding. In contrast, in those with CHF, the organs were not being perfused with blood, not due to lack of blood, but because the heart was unable to propel the blood flow forward [drought and famine in the presence of plenty]. Blood would back up in the lung, the liver, and in the lower extremities. Thus, Stead's group could study the responses of various organs to a spectrum of conditions. Besides this, they uncovered biochemical cascades that accompanied these changes.

Concepts for CHF dating back to the Thorndike days in Boston were pursued. The Thorndike was the research institute with ties to Boston City Hospital, Tufts, and Harvard where Dr.

Stead worked with Soma Weiss, Richard Ebert, and many other great physicians to study the physiology of medical disorders. Attempting to reproduce some of the manifestations of CHF in themselves, Dr. Stead and Dr. Ebert had remained motionless for hours at a time. Leaning against a wall or lying upon a tilt table and drinking loads of salt and water, they were able to reproduce lower extremity swelling, but not the more life-threatening pulmonary edema [lung congestion] much to their chagrin.

Taking on personal risks in the name of science was more common in that day. Dr. Stead actually was a willing subject in one of the first catheterizations at Grady Hospital to make sure it was safe for the patients. Dr. Stead even went through a cardiac catheterization a second time after he was given a small, sterilly-induced, pneumothorax [an air-leak in the lung] to prove a point about venous return to the heart. Initially setting up the catheterization laboratory was full of guesswork. First, the cardiac surgeon, Alfred Blalock [of Blalock-Taussig Shunt fame] suggested that the Office of Scientific Research and Development in Washington would give funds for research projects related to cardiac catheterization studies on heart responses to shock. Next, Dr. James Warren, an essential 'Stead team member', went up to New York to get preliminary directions from Drs. Cournand and Richards on how to run such a laboratory. Finally, the team had to be available and alert, especially on the weekend, when there was a flourish of the ice pick "massacres", camping out for the night in the hospital.

The more the Emory group studied shock, the more they discovered that this constellation of findings resembled CHF. The correlation was truly fortuitous and resulted in concepts that propelled the Emory team and later the Stead's Duke group to the forefront of cardiovascular medicine. There was never a dearth of patients with CHF, even when there were no bloody "massacre" cases.

Stead's catheterization laboratory and the intelligent, inquisitive clinicians who ran or used it: Warren, Brannon, Merrill, or Beeson, opened up whole systems of medical physiology. It was an amazing time. Beeson recalls, "the results were simply spectacular" [23]. Not only was cardiac physiology, diagnosis and therapeutics clarified, but, by repositioning the catheter, the team at Grady unlocked the portals to disordered hepatic, renal, and cerebrovascular difficulties and normal metabolism, as well. Beeson would carry out bacteriologic investigations using this technique, just before the advent of penicillin and would delineate the role of the liver in the clearance of bacteria from the blood. First, the treatment of shock would improve and would antedate another major change: antibiotics, in particular, penicillin, to improve treatment of infections.

In the process of studying patients with CHF in the catheterization laboratory, Arthur Merrill discovered that the blood flowing out of the kidneys had a high concentration of a substance that caused the kidney arteries to clamp down. Dr.

Merrill previously worked with the famous cardiologist, Dr. Tinsley Harrison and developed a renin assay before it became routine for many cardiac and renal problems. They also discovered that the kidney was secreting a substance that was converted into another chemical that would turn out to be an important key to understanding all cardiovascular disorders: angiotensin. The Stead-Merrill team also speculated that there was another important substance in this cascade; that turned out, later, to be aldosterone. So, with the help of a new technique and a focus, Dr. Stead and his 'cathlab' associates started unraveling the mysteries of human physiology. With each physiologic encounter, there was a mysterious missing link. Stead's own probing inquiries and his ability to connect gifted others into a chain reaction of thinking and theorizing provided many medical missing links.

Stead as a Cardiologist

Besides providing the setting for the first **diagnostic** cardiac catheterization spearheaded by Dr. James Warren, Stead used his basement laboratory to reveal the role of the kidney and benefits of diuretics in CHF. "Fluid Dynamics in Congestive Heart Failure", published in *The Archives of Internal Medicine* in 1944 [2], revolutionized our thinking of heart failure and created active controversy regarding concepts like "backward vs. forward failure". His mentor, Dr. Weiss, had studied carotid sinus syncope and beriberi heart disease; Stead and his colleague had studied peripheral circulatory dynamics in Boston. Years later, he would become the editor of the prestigious journal, *Circulation* [see chapter 7]. Dr. James Warren correctly designated him, "a non card-carrying... [and] an unconventional cardiologist" in the journal, *Clinical Cardiology*, 1986 [3]. Eugene Stead was unconventional in many other respects too, evidenced by his administrative skills and, especially, his teaching philosophy.

Dr. Warren was the next in line for the continuation of Stead's cardiovascular creativity. Warren followed Stead for a large portion of the blue-eyed boss's career and was aided at Duke by Dr. Henry McIntosh and others. Dr. Warren directed the cardiac catheterization laboratory at Emory and Duke. At Emory, he was named Chairman of the Department of Physiology but surrendered this position because he preferred clinical work with Dr. Stead. Even when he became Chairman of Medicine at Ohio State, Warren visited Dr. Stead frequently. He, along with Dr. Stead, contributed to their two spouses' heart-healthy cookbook collaborative creation. Stead's association with the cardiovascular system branches into many important tributaries, such as his lasting friendship with Dr. J. W. Hurst, at Emory. Tributes paid to him over the years emphasize a deep cardiac connection.

Translation of Latin phrase: I am an ordinary man [Davus], no solver of riddles like Oedipus.

2

Initial Challenges; **Serpentine Timeline and Biographical Note**

by Robert L. Bloomfield

Knowledge makes the physician, not the name of the school.[22] Paracelsus

ex desuetudina amittuntur privlegia

It may be difficult for the reader to understand the development of Dr. Stead without being a little more familiar with his meandering across the country, especially during his formative years. His maze-like movements, from Georgia to Boston to Cincinnati and back to Boston to Atlanta to Durham, complement his multifaceted nature. Some other environments play a role; New York City, Kerr Lake, the squash court, etc. These wanderings have helped keep Dr. Stead vital and youthful. Though he believed in remaining in the hospital and not traveling to lectures or meetings, once you had an established position, his life in between appointments was anything but settled. His wisdom and perspective stems in part from these outside experiences. Dr. J. Willis Hurst has summarized his history best in a recent interview he conducted with Dr. Stead in the September 1999 issue of *The American Journal of Cardiology* *[1]*.

The interested readers should consult this article, the foreword, as well as the annotated curriculum vitae in this volume, and the references listed at the end of this book. If you have more questions, write me via the publisher. If you still long for more information, you may have the makings of a talented clinician or philosopher. Perhaps we can direct that energy. I think, no, I'm sure that Dr. Stead will add his opinion; quite sure.

Dr. Stead obviously juggled a lot of responsibilities; teaching, administration with its associated politics, clinical work, and family life. What he could not accomplish well by himself, he would delegate to others with more time and undivided talent. Soma Weiss had been correct, Dr. Stead had proven himself as "...a man of achievement." Yet, one person can do only so much. Juggling is a useful skill but, as Dr. Peter Latham warned, juggle one object too many and the whole lot becomes useless; you drop *everything*. One has to know his or her limits without limiting their time for developing useful talents. I know even Dr. Stead had some limits, but, the following chapters will better define them.

The Thorndike

In 1937, when Dr. Stead first reported for his duties with Dr. Weiss at the Thorndike Institute at Boston City Hospital after his residency in Cincinnati, Weiss left for Europe on vacation. In his absence, Dr. Minot, the director of the research laboratories and a famous hematologist, substituted as Stead's chief. Minot was a very finely and narrowly focused person. Stead had interviewed with Dr. Minot as a resident in the past, just one day after Dr. Stead had suffered a squash-match head injury; Dr. Minot had not even mentioned Stead's swollen, bandaged face on that earlier encounter. Minot had microscopic focus and that had helped him discover the cure for pernicious anemia previously. Each morning, Dr. Stead would accompany Dr. Minot into the bathroom and write down the daily list of things to do. This 'to do' list was recited by Minot from behind a partially opened stall door; punctuated and punctual, as he bestrode the commode. Eugene Stead pondered why the Thorndike moved so smoothly and with daily regularity when Dr. Minot was there; it just did. The morning agenda was consistent; everything ran like clockwork with Dr. Minot in charge, discharging duties; case and door closed.

Another senior physician at the Thorndike who impressed Dr. Stead was another hematologist who helped unravel the pernicious anemia/B12 mystery, Dr. Bill Castle. He was an original thinker, not overburdened by research information that he did not need at the moment. There is a word for this ability; he was able to 'compartmentalize' information. Besides, Dr. Castle had a willingness to tackle any clinical problem by drawing information from others with more knowledge. Other people were like books or other ancillary resources to him that he could tap into to solve any difficulty. There is another word for that-'orchestration'. Stead was so impressed with these characteristics that he looked for them in residents and students who worked with him in subsequent years; and they became trademarks of his teaching style. Dr. Castle knew how to rearrange data; not just how to memorize it. He could compose creative variations to manage patient problems without having to know all the answers himself. Bill Castle's methods were some of the first movements of academic medicine and the progression of patient care that became part of Stead's clinical symphony.

The Thorndike, a medical research unit, was part of The Boston City Hospital in association with Harvard and other institutions; Boston City Hospital with the Thorndike was, perhaps, one of the most economically run hospital units in the country. A parsimonious politician ran the place and he let all the residents know, "No lights should be burning after ten o'clock at night." So, Stead followed that directive quite well, for this was a procedure that he had practiced very regularly as a student instructor at Emory; he turned off the lights; a good habit that he still tries to follow today. He was also careful not to bump his head at the top of his tall torso on doorframes in the dark.

Surgical Experiences

After his medical residency, Dr. Stead decided to stay at the Peter Bent Brigham Hospital in Boston to take a surgical internship. He had already obtained some notoriety with the surgical faculty

38

during his previous residency. He was known as the medical resident who had invaded the operating room to confiscate a patient of his that he felt was not being managed correctly. Stead single-handedly picked up the patient from the operating table prior to surgical preparation and carried him back to the ward. He put him back to bed on the ward, laying the patient on his side with a chest tube through the mattress which Stead had previously incised [the head nurse scolded him for ruining a perfectly good mattress]. He then obtained the surgical treatment he felt was better for the patient from a different surgeon.

He learned invaluable lessons from his surgical rotations, though he admits he could never have been a great surgeon; he was not very adept with his hands and he was continually knocking his head on the doorframe when he sauntered into a room, a head he used a great deal. He could work nimbly with his mind and he had a wonderful memory; he could put ideas in new combinations. Yet, he gained a respect for surgeons that translated into an understanding that bridged 'professional' gaps at Emory and Duke. In his sixteen month surgical internship at the Brigham [intern years were longer in those days], he learned to respect surgeons for the amount of time they had to commit to maintain and improve their skills; time that he would rather spend wondering about a case. Surgeons stayed up all night and then had to be ready to operate again at 8:00 the next morning. Because of his surgical tour of duty, Stead never left a lot of patient management orders for the surgeon; if something needed to be carried out, he did it himself. His understanding and respect for surgery aided his negotiations with surgeons at the Duke Medical Center [DUMC] led by Dr. Daryl Hart.

Students understood the difference between learning techniques and gathering data to figure out diagnostic dilemmas. Because of that distinction, the students tended to flock to Stead.

The Peter [Bent Brigham] Principle

Dr. Soma Weiss died in January, 1942 of a ruptured cerebral aneurysm at the youthful age of 42 and Dr. Stead became the acting chairman of the Department of Medicine at The Peter Bent Brigham Hospital in Boston. Dr. Stead loved Boston--the center of the medical world, or so he thought. However, there was a great part of him that longed for his younger days back home in Georgia. He had spent a lot of time in New England, demonstrating to the Harvard students and staff all his acute care experience from Emory; yet he was still a little ill at ease around the old, established Bostonian elite. He even described himself as somewhat "socially inept", though he fit in quite well at tea parties [he hid the fact that he didn't much like parties]. Atlanta may have been less traditional, but there was more need for his expertise down south. There the population was more needy, and he had the chance to prove himself as "a man of achievement" with fewer proprieties, fewer restrictions, perhaps, fewer distractions. If he had stayed in New England, he may have not have been afforded the free rein in academics that allowed him to accomplish what he did.

After being at Emory for a short time his administrative talents gained the attention of the university's trustees and he was pushed into accepting the Deanship. Wearing two, sometimes competing, academic hats was difficult, at best; and it ate up precious time. How could Dr. Stead spend more time on his first loves, clinical work and medical education, with the added new responsibilities? The Peter Principle is similar to juggling too many objects. There were already battles to be waged at the downtown Grady Hospitals. The world war had created problems on the front lines of the wards also. The draft had led to dwindling of the housestaff ranks. Dr. Stead employed tactics to deal with this shortage; upper level medical students did the work of acting interns. The Deanship at Emory produced more proprieties, more restrictions, more distractions. Academic free reign was elusive. He concluded he might not find it in Atlanta.

The Power of Penicillin and The Care of Cortisone

Paul Beeson had been in London at the Red Cross Hospital during the early portion of the war. He was in Boston at the Peter Bent Brigham Hospital with Dr. Stead and he always knew there would be a spot for him there. Before he died, Soma Weiss had told Dr. Beeson to see what Eugene Stead was up to prior to making any decision about accepting an academic appointment.

That he did, and when Dr. Stead offered him a salary of $4000 per year to join him at Emory, Paul moved to Atlanta.

In 1942, penicillin was available, but in short supply. Most of this precious commodity was allocated to the military. Stead, by way of a contact he had in Washington, D.C., arranged for Dr. Beeson to become the 'drug [penicillin] czar' for the entire southeastern region. Not only did this move expose Paul Beeson to the medical community, it helped give him national standing, gave him the opportunity to explore the applications of this important compound, and made it possible for him to save lives.

When Stead moved to Durham, he similarly attached pharmaceutical power to a faculty member on his team, Dr. Frank Engel. Engel, who had accompanied Stead from Emory, was in the Division of Endocrinology under Dr. Stead's direction; he doled out cortisone carefully and had control over the use of this life-saving steroid in the surrounding region. To make these assignments for Beeson and Engel, Stead had to know government people in high and low places.

Engel was a self-made endocrinologist with little formal training in endocrinology; but he was brilliant and absorbed clinical knowledge like a sponge. Beeson was another brilliant physician in many areas, especially in the arena of infectious disease. Stead became known for his cardiovascular expertise before the advent of specialization. These were special times with multiple opportunities; times when there was untapped potential. It was analogous to being a good squash player; you can only

42

anticipate the vicinity where the ball's coming to. Still, you have to be good and ready for it; Dr. Stead was both good and ready to play the game.

An Adaptation of a Biographical Note from Dr. Paul Beeson

Years later, when Dr. Stead officially retired, stepping down triggered many reactions from his colleagues and students, one of which was a symposium in his honor, published by the *Annals of Internal Medicine* in November, 1968 [6]. In that congregation of great physicians, his long-time friend, Paul Beeson, then at Oxford, addressed the gathering with a short biographical note. In that speech he outlined Stead's early serpentine medical wanderings and emphasized Soma Weiss's influence on his development. In particular, he noted both doctors' encouragement of young people and how these people were given medical responsibilities by their stimulating teachers.

Indeed, Drs. Beeson and Stead, themselves were in their youth when so many explosive discoveries affected them, as well as future generations: multiple vascular catheterizations, especially, cardiac, and then, penicillin, better diuretics, a better understanding of congenital heart diseases, renal disorders, shock, anemia, hepatic physiology and CHF. In his speech, Beeson continued to explain how Stead was able to identify exciting and productive people and then to direct them to key clinical questions in their areas of interest. Stead directed their attention to something they had overlooked. He knew how to maximize potentials of both individuals and institutions; Duke presented Stead with many possibilities that Emory could not at mid-century. So, he went north and provided "special growth factors for [many investigators'] academic careers".

In closing, Beeson predicted that Dr. Stead would develop a new interest during his retirement; an interest in delivering good medical services to all people. First, he said, some people needed to listen. "That would be everyone's good fortune, because he is a wise man."

Going to the Chapel

The question remains, 'Why did Stead leave Atlanta?' J. W. Hurst tells us in his book, *The Quest for Excellence [23]*, Stead had become "a legend" after four and a half years at Emory. He had assembled a talented team of physicians. His mentor, Dr. J. Edgar Paullin [see chapter 3], advised him not to move north. Still, an educator needs a university campus to fully mature; the campus was the hub for Stead, like the center of a solar system. Additionally, a campus needs a teacher who can provide stature and brilliance. In his own words, taken from a 1990 correspondence noted in this reference from Hurst, [23, p81], "...in 75 years, Emory will be the dominant southern school, but in my lifetime, Duke will lead the way." Stead gravitated toward Durham.

There were several other forces moving Dr. Stead northward toward the Tarheel State. There was the proximity of the family home to the hospital [no longer would Dr. Stead have to ride the streetcars for miles from Grady hospital to his house]. Now, his children could run through the gardens to meet their father after work. The university and the medical center would be on the same campus. In addition, his salary would climb to $20,000 per year; and he never asked for a raise. The clinics were attached right to the hospital; private and public patients were both seen and considered equal learning opportunities. There were many conveniences, few crimes, and pleasant surroundings.

Best of all, Duke provided Stead with the opportunities to run the hospital, clinics, and medical education programs more or less the way he wanted. He could raise funds as 'free money'; money with few strings attached. Even the funding with strings attached was handled in a way to maximize university growth. The NIH supported medical research efforts if the work could be proven to be *do*able and then accomplished. Stead would have already completed experiments before he applied for the funds. Then he would be guaranteed funds for continuing to do what he had already done and he could pursue something he was already interested in.

The next decade would be a time of NIH expansion; there were many funding opportunities, but they had laid out restrictions. Any new funds had to be applied to uncommitted ventures to encourage university expansion. So, in keeping with those requirements, Stead hired all faculty, even existing faculty, on an uncommitted, yearly basis. By doing this, he was able to

45

conform to the legal stipulation and pay a large portion of salaries with NIH funds; stretching the dollars.

He also ran medical teaching with a different, thoughtful flair. He always showed more deference to the students than to the upper levels of housestaff. Even on rounds, he was kinder and more patient with them than with the residents. When he started attending committee meetings at Duke, he started a new rule; he would not attend any meeting in which students were not allowed. If he were going to attend meetings, which ate into his precious time anyway, then, for goodness sake, at least it would be democratic. Students needed to be more instrumental in patient care, as well. So they were given the responsibility to write initial orders on all patients, even private patients. By unwritten decree, students had to see patients first, before residents, unless an admission was critical. Not only was this democratic, but it was proper for more active learning, despite the resistance from the other physicians in the 'old guard'.

Dr. Stead's methods did not always meet just minimal resistance. Early in his chairmanship at Duke, his premature resignation almost occurred. In frustration, when some of his proposals met resistance, he had delivered his letter of resignation to Dean Davison. When students, housestaff, and colleagues implored him to rescind his letter, he was willing to "eat crow." However, the Dean said the committee would have to vote on it, despite Stead's efforts to remove it from consideration. The tie vote to let him go was broken by one vote in favor of having him stay; by a somewhat paranoid psychiatrist who had gotten to know Dr. Stead on late nights, when they both were roaming the wards either to see patients or avoid certain other people. Dr. Stead, however, did not really avoid anyone ever.

> *The most essential part of a student's instruction is obtained...at the bedside. Nothing seen there is lost; the rhythms of disease are learned by...repetition; ...occurrences stamp themselves indelibly on the memory. Before the student is aware of what he has acquired, he has learned the aspects and causes and probable issue of the diseases he has seen..., and the proper mode of dealing with them...*
> *Oliver Wendell Holmes, Introductory Lecture, 1867 [22]*

Of Rice and Men [and Some Women Too]

When Stead first arrived in Durham in 1947, he was confronted with many jobs in dealing with the physicians who were already there: the 'old guard'. One of them was Dr. Walter Kempner, who was recruited from his homeland in Germany. Kempner was a practitioner with several eccentricities and a huge practice which included many rich and famous patients. He was very strict with his patients, who had to follow the rice diet for months at a time punctuated by urine tests to monitor patient compliance with the dietary restrictions. Dr. Stead recalls Kempner yelling at a nun, "Sister Agnes, you lie, you lie!", after reviewing her urine results; he fell short of rapping her knuckles with a ruler, though he thought about it I'm sure. Perhaps, he changed his physical impulse when he saw her clutch her rosary close to her heart, looking shocked. To say the least, Dr. Kempner was not always a favorite among his colleagues or his patients.

In part, Stead was recruited from Emory to review Kempner's unorthodox clinical methods and records with the hope that Dr. Stead would dismiss Kempner. After reviewing many of his patient records, Dr. Stead was actually impressed with Dr. Kempner's work and recommended that he be retained and promoted to full professorship. He was not the only one at the hospital that was positively impressed. Some of the students and housestaff had noticed that difficult patients of all kinds improved under Dr. Kempner's care. Referring physicians got back their patients with resolved medical problems that they had considered hopeless for many years, problems that were seemingly unrelated to the reason for referral. Many years later, *The Archives of Internal Medicine* [May 1974], [5] would run a series dedicated to Kempner, touting the benefits of the rice diet for many chronic disorders, especially, malignant hypertension. Stead explained that it also improved other vascular disorders, such as hypercholesterolemia, renal diseases, and diabetes.

Kempner's unusual career was supportive of the university and provided Stead with needed funding, probably over $250,000 a year. In the process of getting additional funding from the National Institutes of Health [NIH], the Surgeon General in the early '50s actually resigned in anger, because Stead was able to obtain funds for Kempner, bypassing the customary peer review process. Although future housestaff would question Kempner's credibility, his methods, and his treatment of patients, Dr. Stead remained his friend and supporter. He understood Kempner's non-placebo-controlled studies. On review of the rice diet, the modern reader would have to agree, it has many of the elements of a heart-healthy diet; low in calories, low in fat, protein, and sodium; relatively high in potassium and supplemented with vitamins. Kempner invoked dietary intervention for relatively mild elevations of cholesterol and suggested sound preventive health measures more than fifty years ago.

Dr. Stead believes that Walter Kempner saved more lives of North Carolina adults with medical disorders than any other physician before him and considers him key to garnering the title-"City of Medicine", for Durham. Before Dr. Kempner got embroiled in the many aspects of his rice diet, he spent much of his time with charity cases. Kempner was able to imbue patients that felt hopeless, with a sense of worth and a reason to improve; in many senses he was a 'real doctor'. Stead admits that he always had to be mentally prepared when he faced Kempner, who was a thinker of equal stature to the Chairman of Medicine himself.

Any explanation of Kempner's role deserves mention of Dr. Fred Hanes, Stead's predecessor. He brought Kempner from Germany before Stead's arrival and Kempner represented the international flavor which would set the tone for the future recruitment of excellent medical researchers for Duke. Duke was becoming a nationally and internationally recognized university, not just a regional training ground for local medical personnel, not merely a 'country-club' school.

Also, in the late '40s and early '50s, women were finally being admitted to the medical profession. Years earlier, Oliver Wendell Holmes had voted as dean to get Harvard to agree to admit females to the medical school. He was rebuffed and females were not admitted to Harvard Medical School until 1945. Dr. Stead's institution was already in step; as a matter of fact, they were racing ahead. Their first woman chief resident, Dr. Grace P. Kerby was 'anointed' [for want of a better term] for the 1950-51 housestaff class, which was 15% female. Dr. Arthur Finn, one of our commentators below, recalls, "She was stern of visage, tall and lanky, and smiled rarely. We thought she was amazing, always around, and wondered if she ever went home." She had been an intern previously in 1948 and also had done a dermatology residency at Duke. Gender did not make the difference at Stead's hospital; race or religion were not supposed to be issues either; Dr. Stead had always made an effort to desegregate any hospital he worked in, whether in Atlanta, Boston, Cincinnati or Durham. Church affiliations which tended to limit the applicant pools of both students and housestaff were terminated or minimized at most distinguished medical universities at that time.

Dr. Stead recalls that Kerby was one of the very best chief residents he ever had. Later, she replaced the departed Dr. John Hickam, a close ally of Stead, in the faculty position of housestaff education director. It was rumored that she could drink any male under the table. She retired after Dr. Stead stepped down; retiring, in part, because of her diminishing hearing.

Another essential woman in Dr. Stead's academic career was Bess M. Cebe. She was there as his faithful secretary six months after Eugene Stead arrived at Duke; and she filled that role for twenty-six years, until the chairman's voluntary retirement. He arrived from Atlanta with Drs. Hickam, Myers, and Engel. The first two both had offices down the hall from their chief. Bess, John Hickam, and Jack Myers moved almost like an inseparable unit, wherever the university felt they should call home base. Bess's job was to pick up the things that Stead and his teammates dropped during their juggling acts.

Anyone involved in hospital work knows that a major medical center can not run at all smoothly without the coordination provided by the devoted secretaries. The team of Stead-Cebe allowed Dr. Stead to pursue teaching rounds three times each week, morning report six days every week, meetings with division chiefs, reviewing every research manuscript emanating from his department, attending clinics, executing administrative responsibilities; and all from behind the same desk he was given in 1947.

Early Articles

An interest with the peripheral circulation was shared between Stead and his mentor, Soma Weiss. In 1939, in the *Journal of Clinical Investigation*, [29] these two colleagues collaborated on a study on the peripheral circulation. In that publication, they noted that the vasculature, as opposed to the heart, was more sensitive to noxious agents. They also observed that patients symptoms varied depending on whether or not the subject was tired or rested. Stead's concern with the cardiovascular system, autonomic nerve effects, patient symptoms, and the organism's individual response to stress was already apparent.

A similarity in the peripheral signs of CHF and shock was emphasized in Stead's 1942 article with Richard Ebert in the *Archives of Internal Medicine [30]*. This concept was soon after reiterated in the surgical literature in the *Archives of Surgery [31]*. Within this article, they enumerate basic mechanisms for heart failure, including pericardial tamponade [keeping the heart from filling adequately-see above in Ice(pick) Age section, chapter 1], pulmonary thromboembolism [impeding outflow from the heart], and metabolic disorders [non-cardiovascular causes]. All these different causes for CHF, Stead felt, represented a fertile area for many studies from many fields; even those distant from cardiology [32].

By 1949, Stead had enough data to relate CHF to secondary problems in renal blood flow and resulting kidney disorders in the *American Journal of Medicine [33]*. A review of Stead's C.V., reveals his continued effort and persistence to explain this proven group of concepts through the following decade.

The Role of Medical Research

Ah! In Durham, one can appreciate a combination of smells wafting through the humid, thick air: warm pine needles, tobacco [cough], formaldehyde from the anatomy labs, and other reagents [cough, cough]. The development of medical research at Duke has a connection with the sultry weather, so well-accepted in the South. When Stead settled in the Tarheel State, only the operating rooms had the necessary air conditioning; and even these were only a few degrees Centigrade cooler than the below-ground level offices at the black Grady. Even the elementary research that Stead was conducting required steady, temperate temperatures if controlled conditions were going to be maintained. If the thermometer reached 90 degrees, the seal that coated the stopcocks in laboratory test tubes popped out and studies were ruined or made impossible. Air conditioning made experimentation a potential reality; and when it was added to the Private Diagnostic Clinic, air conditioners improved the non-laboratory efficiency there, as well. Thus, advantages for one section or department bled over and benefited another area. Other resources from the Department of Medicine were used to support related ventures from those sympathetic Basic Science Departments, such as Biochemistry. It was from these non-clinical departments that teachers for medical students were recruited. One of these teachers was Philip Handler.

Dr. Philip Handler was a fine biochemist and teacher. He has been credited with helping Stead develop the Research Training Program [RTP] at the medical center. He shared some of the characteristics with Dr. Stead that made them both effective leaders. They were great 'raconteurs' [I can attest to the fact that Dr. Stead still is] and perceptive talent scouts. Their story-telling skills helped make them great and inspiring teachers. Stories can be an effective means of communicating with students and patients. Dr. Stead still believes that by attaining a patient's off-the-cuff story, the clinician may garner much useful information that the systematic clinical history may not provide. Handler's and Stead's shared ability to spot gifted individuals with medical 'promise' and of future 'achievements' distinguishes them as builders of programs and university departments. As a duo, Handler and Stead identified and fueled the hiring of Dan Tosteson as the Chairman of the Department of Physiology. He was a gifted physician/researcher who wad later recruited by Harvard.

Phil Handler shared several other characteristics with Eugene Stead. One of them was foresight; he was the first other department chairman who shared Dr. Stead's vision of institutional development. Handler moved his entire department of biochemists out of the old medical school building cluster. In doing so, he was able to expand earlier than other basic science departments.

The RTP was another Stead strategy to join seemingly disparate disciplines in the pursuit of improved health care for patients and university growth far beyond the Duke Gardens. The M.D. students could gain research knowledge by applying themselves in a laboratory setting related to clinical medicine and do enough required work to obtain a Ph.D. degree. 'Mudfuds', as they were affectionately called ['or as some have renamed them-the methylene Blue Devils'], became an integral part of the medical team. The concept flourished, even after Dr. Handler left to become the president of the National Academy of Sciences. 'Muds' were known as medical team members that got their hands dirty from their clinical duties; 'Phuds' were thought of as those who got their minds dirty. The combination to promote the idea of the 'thinking doc' seemed appropriate and timely; these doctors were on the 'cutting edge' of medical-research.

Key faculty members participating in the RTP included Jim Wyngaarden, as well as Dan Tosteson. Dan, as noted above, came to Duke as Chairman of the Physiology Department and eventually became the Dean of Harvard Medical School. He adopted Dr. Handler's position at Duke when the latter left Durham for Washington. Dr. Wyngaarden directed the RTP and left Durham to become Chairman of Medicine at the University of Pennsylvania. He returned to Duke, superceding Dr. Stead as the Chairman of the Department of Medicine.

Starship Commander 'Blue Eyes': We must keep our team on a high state of alert. Engage.

First Officer Wyngaarden: Red Alert!; We should increase output from our allies in the far quadrant of the university–the mighty mitochondria.

Engineer McIntosh: The patient's tachyarrythmia is reaching warp speed. I don't think the boosters will hold her, Cap'n.

Dukies Win by a Fieldgoal with Help From Florida Gators

One of the previous chief residents designated by Dr. Stead, Robert Whalen, became a noted cardiologist. He and others, such as Dr. Henry McIntosh [see chapter 4] under Stead's direction solved a medical mystery that had been puzzling cardiologists for years; an entity referred to as 'hypertrophic subaortic stenosis'. Dr. Whalen solved it during a dynamic time when the Beatles were popular and films were full of futuristic action; recall *2001* by Stanley Kubrick. Cineangiography [moving pictures of blood vessels, especially around the heart] and similar techniques were revealing new truths about cardiac physiology. Now, under dynamic conditions with the heart beating on film, [not in time to the British rock music beat] one could actually see a constricting band of cardiac muscle under the aortic heart valve interfering with the blood flow. The physician could even make the test more 'true-to-life' by infusing isoproteronol [an epinephrine-like drug] intravenously. Then, one could capture the dynamic emergence of this obstruction to flow on videotape along with data demonstrating a pressure change on both sides of this band. Yet, there were not enough patients to explore this phenomenon; nor were all the proposed investigations appropriate for patients.

What the cardiologists needed was an animal model to pursue more studies; and they found it in the vicinity of the first Tarzan movies and only a few hundred miles from the underwater beauties, the Wiki Watchi Girls; the animals were alligators, some of them up to six feet long, from Silver Springs,

Florida. In Florida, people had viewed nature's wonders through glass bottom boats, and as an added attraction, tourists could gawk at synchronized swimmers under the crystal clear water. In Durham, not a favorite tourist spot, they were using video monitors, tape players, and cardiac catheters, to view the secrets of the human body and improve a patient's cardiac output. It turned out that the prenatal development of the alligator heart made these creatures prone to demonstrate a similar problem. Alligators spend time swimming or resting with their snouts above water or underwater, even for hours at a time. The alligator heart incorporates subvalvular [below the aortic valve] rings in cardiac muscle to divert blood to an air sac for extracting oxygen for extended periods of submersion under water. For more physiologic details, the reader is directed to a reference [8] at the end of this book; an article by McIntosh, Morris, Whalen, et. al.

With the aid of those 'gators', Stead's group unraveled that cardiac conundrum to the delight of the medical community; by studying physiology with a new technology and applying biological to medical science. After evaluating this phenomenon, these doctors did not take extra vacation time and go to Disneyworld to celebrate their successes of Olympic proportion. They just stayed in Durham, listening to the chirping of the cicadas in the evenings, to perfect their 'triple Lutz' or some other fine technical skill of blade and blood vessel.

Chair for a Day

Dr. Wilburt Cornell ['Dave'] Davison, the Dean of Duke Medical Center, like Dr. Stead, was adept as a fundraiser. He had obtained a large contribution from a generous benefactor, Ms. Florence P. McAlister, in the late '40s. The sum was enough to create a 'chair' in the Department of Medicine. However, when Ms. Florence P. called one afternoon to say she was coming to the hospital for a visit, she expressed a small misunderstanding; she was coming by to see the actual chair!!

Not wishing to disappoint her, Dr. Davison immediately sprung into action. He called a local furniture producer and had them manufacture a fine chair; good enough to serve as a throne. On the front of the upright portion was a golden plaque engraved with the letters: THE FLORENCE P. MCALISTER CHAIR.

Years later, after Dr. Stead retired, Dr. Roscoe Robinson, the head of the renal section, attempted to take the chair with him to Vanderbilt in Tennessee, but Dr. Stead convinced the well-known nephrologist to just try and replace the actual chair; Stead himself carried the throne down the hall from the office to protect it from Dr. Robinson's clutches. Trying to replace this piece of memorabilia proved to be too expensive an endeavor for the Tennessee-bound titan and to this day, that 'chair' remains in the Chairman [or, soon, Chairwoman] of Medicine's office in Durham.

The Golden Years and The Sponge vs. Survey Modes

Dr. Stead considered the internship and residency years, the golden years; impressionable times when very intelligent men and women were ripe repositories for medical memories. These were formative years when young doctors might gain or lose interest in a certain medical or surgical area of specialization. These years would shape the future conduct of young physicians; and in the process, when the resident was climbing high on the learning curve [not the forgetting one-see below], he or she was a ripe repository for many points of view. At the peak of absorbing information, residents were ready to adapt, ready to alter their track, and, at times, ready to extricate themselves from their previous intentions, their previous goals, their previous dreams.

Stead still believes in the 'forgetting curve': the young physician in practice forgets much of the information he or she learned in medical school, if they don't continually apply it. Since Stead invoked the forgetting curve concept [see front cover], the good educators under his direction had a major responsibility of making the internship and residency truly 'Golden Years'. The clinical teachers would give their juniors a lot of useful information, so that even after they left academia and could be on the downswing of the forgetting curve [see cover], the graduate of this program would be a good physician. Dr. Stead taught the student to continue learning from each clinical experience. The higher up you were on the 'forgetting curve' when you graduated medical school, the more you would probably retain years later, regarding clinical information.

The residents had some responsibilities also. To become good clinicians, they were expected to get out of solely the 'sponge mode' and be capable of switching to the 'survey mode'. In the sponge mode, they would soak up a lot of data; in the survey mode they would analyze data, reorganize data, and evaluate the clinical value of data. They would learn to think; they would learn to reapply what they had learned in another area of medicine to new patient problems. Problem-solving skills would improve from repetition.

An Empire and a Stately Building

The emperor in the old tale may have had no clothing, but he may well have had a hospital gown and wielded an antique stethoscope. Stead was a more observant emperor, who was well aware that outward appearances need tending to. Old habits are often like good old stories; they die hard. This is especially true when the old habits involve old buildings. An old building at a university connotes prestige and when you're competing with the Ivy League [sometimes referred to as the oi vay league], you're at a disadvantage if your college buildings don't even have ivy! Thus, it was a difficult task to introduce changes in the structures that defined Duke, modeled, in part, after Princeton; but change was essential. Change was part of the blueprint for the university expansion that Stead, the educator, had in mind; he had to break some old habits.

The approach to the patient with the illness was at the foundation of the potential expansion. Other departments in the basic sciences were becoming involved in clinical research. There just wasn't room for all these folks in the present buildings. Promising researchers were even renovating space; converting old bathrooms into laboratories by themselves with help from a local hardware store. A multifaceted approach required new space and new buildings to house a more extensive faculty.

Expansion was made possible initially with 'free money' generated by the Private Diagnostic Clinic [PDC]. The PDC offered Stead a fine forum for teaching on private patients, as well as being a steady financial source. Along with the Anna H. Hanes Fund, Dr. Stead had created perhaps the most influential and best endowed medical chairmanship "in the whole world", as Dr. David T. Smith, a colleague, stated.

Dr. Stead and his faithful secretary, Ms. Cebe, left two offices when they moved into new quarters at Duke. This space became the cardiac catheterization laboratory, run by Warren and McIntosh. They still needed space to house the cardiovascular division at Duke Medical Center. Dr. Warren's associate, Dr. McIntosh, had a late-night inspiration at 2:00 a.m. as he was voiding. Great notions and vagal impulses tend to hit one in those 'wee wee' hours. He put on his overalls and did some spelunking in the dark. The crawl space under the old offices was spacious, vacant, and in need of renovation; the subterranean 'Durhamites' were colonizing far and wide. 'Eureka!', [not uremia], Henry had found it!; and he knew whom to ask for 'free money' to develop the space.

Dr. McIntosh also expanded the space needed for their mammalian and reptilian partners by building five miles off campus at the animal farm, with Stead's blessing and watchful eye. Physiologic studies were carried out there by many university departments; and you thought that film, *Animal House,* took place at Dartmouth!

When eons have past, I predict that archaeologists of the future will find bits of ancient research facilities in the fertile, humid forest that was once Durham, where lemurs roamed and femurs were repaired. Digging deeply into the hard red clay, they may unearth the three vases of Eve, each characterized by a fusiform enlargement at their base-'vasodilatation'. Cataloguing items from Dr. Stead's ancient tomb and office, they may also discover a few antique lamps, as well. They will then find a fossilized catheter from the 'Steadian Dynasty' and will rejoice rather than express dismay at their lack of unearthing a mere Ming Vase; oy, vase mir!!, enough with these old antics.

Translation of Latin phrase: By disuse are privileges lost.

3

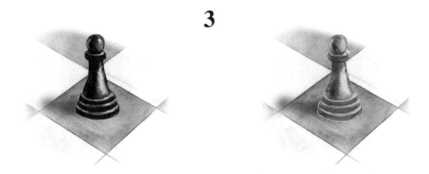

Setting Up the Board; **Mentors, Colleagues, and Students**
by Robert L. Bloomfield

*Common sense in matters medical is rare, and is
usually in inverse ratio to the degree of education. [22]*
Sir William Osler

fructu non foliis arborem aestima

Before Stead even considered medicine as a career, he had
contact with that profession by way of the family's physician, Dr.
J. Edgar Paullin. Dr. Paullin was trained in Baltimore, taught by
Osler at Johns Hopkins, schooled at Emory, and was a very well-
respected practitioner in Atlanta and the entire southeastern U. S.
It is rumored that Paullin inherited Osler's actual stethoscope,
receiving it from his teacher when he completed his training.
When Dr. Stead attended the medical school at Emory and later,
became the Chairman of Medicine, he continued his friendship

with his former doctor and teacher. One day the cigarettes, the ashtrays, and the matches had disappeared from Paullin's home. Stead expressed surprise and asked Paullin what had brought on this dramatic change. Apparently, Paullin was impressed by his young, loving granddaughter. As he was tossing her up in the air one day, she commented, "Grandpa, what makes you wheeze so loudly?" He put the child down gently, walked into his house, disposed of all the cigarettes and never smoked again.

Gene Stead's mentor was also impressed with his pupil and took a deep breath; he sighed without a wheeze and concluded that his pupil's stature had exceeded expectations.

Drs. Henry Asbury Christian, Joe Aub, and Sam Levine

During the presidential address that Dr. Stead gave at the meeting of the American Society for Clinical Investigation in 1953, in which he described Soma Weiss's influence, he made note of another great influence, his second chief, Dr. Henry Christian [6]. Dr. Henry Christian was the Chief of Medicine at the Brigham before Soma Weiss accepted that post. Christian stimulated the pursuit of scholarship and academic initiative in the brightest recruits from all over the country. He taught Stead, among other things, that motivated students can better themselves in spite of the shortcomings of the faculty. Henry Christian was one of academic medicine's great teachers and was on the very top of the traditional university pyramid. Dr. Christian pushed the academic envelope; considering teaching philosophy, it appears that Dr. Weiss, going beyond this, broke it open.

Dr. Christian joined Harvey Cushing at Harvard in 1912. They had both been recruited from Johns Hopkins to be chairmen of the Department of Medicine and of Surgery, respectively, at the Brigham. They both agreed to retire early, and arranged with the Dean of Harvard Medical School to step down from their posts at age 63. Christian left his post without incident, but Cushing tried to stay, because he felt he was as adept a surgeon as ever. Still, the Dean would not rescind the agreement. Cushing got angry and took his library and his other valuable accoutrements to Yale where they treated him more to his liking. Dr. Stead repeated their examples years later and retired at even an earlier age [age-60]; and he left 'Durham-town' for a year, voluntarily, without a quarrel to give the new chairman, Dr. Wyngaarden, a chance to fortify his position.

In Stead's day, the Boston hospitals required intern applicants to appear in person for an interview. On the long bus ride from Atlanta to Boston, Stead had read the recently published book, The Heart, by Paul Dudley White. In it was a chapter on coarctation of the aorta, a condition that was new to young Stead and rarely seen by those more experienced within the medical community. His chief examiner at the interview at Peter Bent Brigham Hospital was Dr. Sam Levine, a cardiologist of great distinction. Dr. Levine had recently cared for a patient with congenital occlusion of the aortic arch and wondered if Dr. Stead was familiar with this rare condition. Stead had just reviewed that problem in White's book and was capable of satisfying all of Levine's questions regarding this disease. In the end, Levine recommended that the Brigham offer Stead an internship, which was promptly accepted.

As time progressed at the Brigham, young Gene Stead spent more time with a physician who made scientific investigation and current research integral in his practice, Dr. Joseph Aub. Housestaff members were intimidated to some degree by the austere chief, Dr. Christian. Dr. Aub, more easily approachable, was a basic scientist engaged in the study of patients with cancer and endocrine disorders. Aub asked Stead the kind of questions that one couldn't answer by consulting books. He was impressed by all his medical teachers, though he remained closest to Dr. Aub over the years.

After his medical internship, residency, Stead pursued another apprenticeship for sixteen months in surgery under the stewardship of Dr. Elliot Cutler, at the Brigham. Dr. Cutler knew of Stead's reputation as a patient advocate and was glad to have him in the surgical program. Many physicians-in-training might consider this obsessive, but Stead enjoyed further patient care. He was exceptional as he took another internship with no interest or intention of even becoming a surgeon. His parents expressed some concerns; why was their son, 'the doctor' still in training and not settling down to a lucrative practice. Well, at least they could beam; he was at Harvard; but, why was he such a slow learner?; he wasn't getting any younger, oi!

Blackenhorn

One fine evening, sometime after his internships in 'Beantown', MA, Dr. Stead was taking a steamy shower across the way from his research laboratory at The Thorndike. Young Dr. Stead met a young medical professor who, by chance, peered over the adjacent stall; he shook Stead's hand and informed him that the chairman of medicine from Cincinnati was seeking someone from outside the training program there to be chief resident. Dr. Stead took that job after working out the details of that move to the Midwest; which included providing for his brother Bill's medical education at Emory.

Stead became the chief resident for Dr. Marion Blackenhorn at Cincinnati General where he obtained more clinical responsibilities than even he had imagined; he jumped off of the surrounding research rocks and onto the red hot clinical coals-'ouch'! He actually noted more heat stroke cases in them-thar hills [Ohio?] than he saw down south [28]. Apparently, the heat was more oppressive in the tall tenement buildings in Cincinnati than in the open meadows of the South.

During his time in Ohio, Dr. Soma Weiss came from Boston to round with Stead as a Visiting Professor. They were both impressed with each other. When Soma departed, he called back and suggested that Stead return to Boston as a research fellow under him at The Thorndike. The salary Weiss offered was $1200 per year; Stead requested $1800. Soon thereafter, Stead got a wire from Dr. Weiss later, stating they had found the needed additional funding-"Found $1800." Stead wired Weiss back, "See you in July."

The Cincinnati chief residency lasted eighteen months; they really got their money's worth for resident labor back in the '30s. In that stint, Stead learned much about bedside teaching and he gained clinical confidence in running a busy hospital service. He was freer than previously at working out his own ideas and, during those months, he learned more about delegating responsibilities to other members of the healthcare team. Dr. Blackenhorn gave Dr. Stead a lot of room to grow as a physician. By the way, his brother Bill did well in the medical field as well; he made his name in infectious diseases and became known as 'Mr. Tuberculosis', from his work at the Arkansas State Health Department. [Didn't someone else named Bill write: "T.B. or not T.B...."?]

Soma Weiss

Soma Weiss, born in Hungary, was Dr. Stead's fifth and final chief. But, he left a lasting impression. At age 39, he was named Hersey Professor of the Theory and Practice of Physic at Harvard and Physician-in-Chief to the Peter Bent Brigham Hospital. Stead accompanied Weiss to the Brigham, after working with him at the Thorndike. Dr. Weiss was a charismatic leader who stimulated young doctors and students at Harvard. He was the first university appointed medical chief of the Jewish faith. His popularity among residents was meant to aid the Brigham in regaining that hospital's prior top standing in the medical education system.

Dr. Weiss encouraged housestaff and students to accept clinical responsibilities as a means of learning medicine. He promoted the teaching of younger staff as a means of uncovering the shortcomings of upper-level staff members, thus broadening both faculty groups' knowledge bases. Gene Stead benefited from this approach, learning from what is not known. The skepticism and new approach provided by the 'untarnished' student was a boon to the instructor of medicine. This way of teaching as a learning device became a trademark of Stead chairmanships.

Dr. Soma Weiss taught that rank could be an artificial barrier in the transfer of knowledge; actually, a junior member of the rounding team may have the most valuable information or the freshest approach to a chronic medical problem. Respect was given to those with a thirst for understanding, not, necessarily, for seniority alone.

The role of research, in this medical scheme of things, was secondary to some other goals; a mindset that Stead adopted. The output of research was subordinate to training students and residents, for improving the thinking of the housestaff and for improving the teaching from older clinicians. Teaching the practice of medicine was, in turn, always subordinate to caring for the patient.

Dr. Weiss always retained a great interest in the patient's presenting complaints; he stressed accurate assessment of each symptom. Still, there was another secret that Dr. Stead learned from studying with Soma. The secret of running a successful medical department; which is to surround yourself with talented, energetic clinicians, "... [m]any of whom outdistance [their chief] in some field." [6]. These are some of the 'secrets' Stead took with him wherever he went; and they provided him with tremendous, daily satisfaction as he watched his staff members grow.

Progression of Mentors

A perfunctory analysis of Stead's chiefs reveals an evolution that may provide some clues to understanding Dr. Stead's development. Dr. Paullin was a fine practitioner and a learned individual who taught current knowledge. Dr. Christian also did this as well, but was closer to discoveries and new knowledge in medicine. It seems that Dr. Aub was closer to new data still. Christian "fostered ... initiative" in his residents and gave "honor to scholarship"; he "expected his residents to produce". Dr. Cutler worked long hours and was "loved and honored" by all the staff. Stead's clinical skills were honed and fortified in Cincinnati by Dr. Marion Blackenhorn. Dr. Blackenhorn gave all his residents a "very free hand in running the service" and taught them how to delegate responsibilities.

However, it was Dr. Weiss who pulled it all together. He stressed current medical practice, new knowledge [even that in the German literature], teaching to all levels of students, and the

70

importance of undergraduate pupils, as well. He was aware of the physician's own ignorance and attempted to eradicate barriers that interfered with learning. Teaching was a great learning tool for faculty members and ward rounds, near bedsides, was and remained a communal experience for the spectrum of students and residents.

To Soma Weiss, the production of clinical research was important in that it served as a stimulus to improve thinking; it remained a means of keeping mature minds agile. But, the basis for all this thinking was the patient's symptoms; complaints of not feeling normal; feelings that can try the patience of doctors trained in 'what is known'.

Parallel to Stead's famed 'Sunday School' in Atlanta and Durham, Weiss had conducted 'Tuesday Night Teaching' [not all you can eat fried fish nite] at Boston City Hospital, years before. What came across in any presentation he delivered was the sense that he really enjoyed doing whatever he did. He liked dealing with people, whether they were hospital patients or the "Irish politician who ran the Boston City Hospital." He bathed, not in his own limelight, but in the triumphs, both great and small, of his less confident students. He turned a student's shortcoming or a trainee's tentativeness into an asset. When Stead's mother used the phrase, "He's just a slow learner." to rationalize Stead's prolonged training to inquisitive others, Dr. Weiss replied, "You know she might be right." Being a slow learner allows you to discover what others may have missed.

71

The following individuals are listed in Dr. G. Wagner's book as physicians that became chairman and chiefs elsewhere and were trained initially by Dr. Stead:

1. Paul B. Beeson: Chairman, Medicine, Emory; to Chairman, Medicine, Yale; to Radcliffe Infirmary, England; to Seattle VA Hospital
2. Ivan L. Bennett: Chairman, Pathology, Johns Hopkins; to Vice-president, New York University Medical School
3. Kenneth Blaylock: Chairman, Dermatology, Virginia
4. Morton D. Bogdonoff: Chairman, Medicine, Abraham Lincoln School of Medicine; to Executive Associate Dean and Professor of Medicine, Cornell, NYC
5. Stuart Bondurant: Chairman, Medicine, Albany Medical College; to Dean, Albany Medical College, NY
6. Rubin Bressler: Chairman, Pharmacology, Arizona; to Chairman, Medicine, Arizona
7. C. Hilmon Castle: Chairman, Family and Community Medicine, Utah
8. Leighton Cluff: Chairman, Medicine, University of Florida at Gainesville; to Robert Wood Johnson Foundation
9. William P. Deiss: Chairman, Medicine, Texas at Galveston
10. Richard V. Ebert: Chairman, Medicine, Minnesota
11. E. Harvey Estes: Chairman, Community Health Sciences, Duke
12. Abner Golden: Chairman, Pathology, Kentucky
13. Sidney Grossberg: Chairman, Microbiology, Medical College of Wisconsin
14. John B. Hickam: Chairman, Medicine, Indiana
15. Bernard C. Holland: Chairman, Psychiatry, Emory
16. Wallace R. Jensen: Chairman, Medicine, George Washington, to Chairman, Medicine, Albany Medical College
17. David Kipnis: Chairman, Medicine, Washington University
18. William H. Knisley: Chairman, Institute of Biology & Medicine, Michigan State, to Vice-Chancellor for Health Affairs, Texas; to President, Medical University of South Carolina
19. Peter O. Kohler: Chairman, Medicine, Arkansas

20. James Leonard: Chairman, Medicine, Pittsburg
21. Samuel P. Martin: Chairman, Medicine, Florida at Gainesville; to Wharton School of Finance, Pennsylvania
22. Henry D. McIntosh: Chairman, Medicine, Baylor College of Medicine, Houston, Texas
23. Charles Mengel: Chairman, Medicine, Missouri
24. A. Donald Merritt: Chairman, Genetics, Indiana
25. H. Victor Murdaugh: Chairman, Medicine, South Carolina
26. Jack D. Myers: Chairman, Medicine, Pittsburg; to University Professor, Pittsburg
27. Joseph C. Ross: Chairman, Medicine, South Carolina
28. Peritz Scheinberg: Chairman, Neurology, Miami
29. Theodore B. Schwartz: Chairman, Medicine, Rush-Presbyterian
30. James V. Warren: Chairman, Medicine, Texas at Galveston; to Chairman, Medicine, Ohio State
31. Arnold M. Weissler: Chairman, Medicine, Wayne State, MI
32. James B. Wyngaarden: Chairman, Medicine, Duke

The following are department or section chairmen in other institutions that were trained by Dr. Stead and are not noted from the source above:

1. Philip Bondy, became Chief of Endocrinology at Yale University
2. Earl N. Metz, became Chief of Hematology at Ohio State University
3. Bert W. O'Malley, became Chief of Biochemistry at Yale
4. Roscoe R. Robinson, became Chairman of Medicine at Vanderbilt University, Florence P. McAllister Chair of Medicine after Dr. Stead
5. J. Graham Smith, became Chief of Dermatology at University of Georgia Medical Center in Augusta

Promoting Duke

Reading through this impressive list of clinicians and 'Steadmen', one is struck by the variety of disciplines represented by these former associates of Dr. Stead; pathology, pharmacology, community medicine, neurology, psychiatry, dermatology, microbiology, and genetics. Not only was Stead spreading these 'ambassadors' to distant institutions in medicine and related areas, he was gaining extensive free advertising for his program in North Carolina.

While he was spreading the word across the nation, Stead was also concentrating his resources in the Triangle area. By doing so, he was increasing his armamentarium in Chapel Hill and Raleigh and attempting to stimulate growth at Research Triangle Park; healthy competition was transformed into health care cooperation. At one time he even suggested that some of the knowledgeable scientists from the NIH relocate down south; 'come on down and setup shop for a spell.'

His approach to the kind of research condoned by the NIH was also somewhat unorthodox. He did not believe, as one was taught in basic science class by experts, that every potential treatment required a randomized, controlled study. It did not always make sense to him, because it assumed all the subjects were more similar to each other than he believed people really are.

Stead was convinced that there were subtle biases even in getting the grants initially. Those people who decided on funding were sure, in Gene's view, that you could only draw rational conclusions from randomized trials.

The following is taken from Dr. John Laszlo's manuscript, *The Doctor's Doctor [28],* and is adapted from his interview with Dr. Stead:

> *It was rumored that I wrote my grants by stating in the application only that "next year I'm going to do more of what I did last year." ...there was no truth to that.... ... 90% of what I proposed to do in my grant requests were things we had already done. We ... took these projects out of papers that were going to be published [in] six months .... we were awarded money based on what we said we would do and had already ... completed what we promised to do, then we had the freedom to do what we wanted. ... one of my rules was never to take money for anything I didn't want to do. ... if you really want to do something, you'll do it whether you have the money for it or not.*
> *Eugene Stead*

In that same manuscript, Dr. Stead, 'raconteur extraordinaire' that he is, tells a story of a physicist that used the same funding strategy. He, apparently, applied for a grant, but when it underwent peer-review, the committee denied his grant because they were positive the experiment couldn't possibly be done. Boy, were they wrong.

A Talk With Colleagues About Their Future
And Beginner's Luck

When Dr. Stead accepted his many awards, his acceptance speeches resembled those one sees each year at the Academy Awards; "I'd like to thank everyone who made this possible-the janitor who cleans up the vomit from the ward floor at night [aside]: [they really, really like me; or do they really, really fear me.]" Osler said that humility was the characteristic which lent permanence to other essential qualities of clinical greatness. Well, Dr. Stead demonstrated that throughout his career. He gave much credit for his success to junior members of his team, as well as to nurses and other ancillary hospital personnel. He avoided adding his name to papers if he was not playing an active role in the actual study. Even today, he credits the excellent support system he was afforded by his wife, Evelyn, his children, and his colleagues in his lifelong quest for superior healthcare.

A career in medicine is demanding. His advice to young colleagues starting out was: enjoy your professional life as you go and make little distinction between work and play. Perhaps, he assumed the trainees were as dedicated as he was. Your years following medical school are supposed to be the freest you will have. Make them satisfying and live below your income, he would say to them. He would also encourage housestaff to be students of human behavior and teach that brain structure limits people's personal growth. Those people with the most flexible and advanced brains, though, should be expected to meet the highest requirements; others we should accept or, at least, tolerate. Throughout his chairmanships, Dr. Stead promoted the best qualities of his associates, while minimizing their shortcomings.

Dr. Stead found that letting younger colleagues flex their academic muscles and execute their ideas and express their independence had several advantages. Dr. J. Willis Hurst has described the barriers to free thinking when ideas have been established from previous instruction. Dr. Hurst warns that an individual told not to think of a *white bear*, will, in fact, not be able to stop thinking about a *white bear*; something he labels "the White Bear Syndrome". Colleagues beginning their careers in medicine were not locked into a particular line of thinking; their minds were open and they could more easily follow the neuronal path 'less traveled'.

Having more alternative channels to traverse, the beginner could solve a complex problem or clinch an elusive diagnosis. To paraphrase Stead, we all need to recycle information, look at a situation through the eyes of our colleagues, remove our prejudices and avoid traps set for *white bears*.

Jack Myers and The Crew

Myers and Stead met at the Brigham in 1939; it was the day Hitler bombed Poland. Jack Myers had also been a resident under Paul Beeson in Atlanta and was recruited from California's Stanford University; a protegé of Dr. Arthur Bloomfield. He had been in active duty with the Brigham-Harvard army unit headed by the Harvard surgeon, Dr. Elliot Cutler. After Beeson came to Atlanta to work with Stead, Jack Myers joined them where he became chief of medicine at the VA hospital. In 1947, Myers went north to become part of the Duke contingent.

Dr. Myers had a very orderly approach to medicine. He could absorb and juggle an immense amount of clinical data, so that he could diagnose and manage cases that others could not. He became known at DUMC as the clinician that diagnosed correctly a case at a conference [CPC] that had stumped every other doctor; a case of tularemia ['rabbit fever']. While this is amazing, remember what Dr. Stead observed; whoever saw the patient last, would have the best notes [and assessment], because they had the advantage of everyone else's distilled thoughts and the passage of more time. None of this minimizes Jack Myers' great achievements.

Myers expected a lot; he ran a tight ship and could 'whip' any resident into shape; 'Fort Myers' was a logical stop for inductees into the DUMC 'boot camp'. Stead recalls that shortage of space at Duke in those early years might lead to classes meeting in ward corridors. Jack, at those times, might bellow, "Clear the hall." If Myers had a point to make, he'd pound the table in his dogmatic fashion and accept little argument; "This is the way it is." John Hickam, the perpetual diplomat, would 'soften up' many of the problems that arose with Jack.

This distinction paralleled the development of medical students. Up until the time of junior residency from the second year of medical school, students would tend to identify with Jack Myers; after that, they would identify more closely with the scholarly Drs. Engel or Hickam. Each faculty member had his vital role in the educational process. Frank Engel and John Hickam were two of the most scholarly people that Dr. Stead had the pleasure of working with. Stead was probably personally most fond of Hickam, who died unexpectedly at the age 56 from a bleed in the brain like that suffered by Dr. Soma Weiss. Dr. Myers went on to chair the Department of Medicine at the University of Pittsburgh School of Medicine. He took four Duke faculty members with him. In Stead's words, "Jack was ready for his own show."

Dr. John Hickam, another in the clinical 'troika plus', a vital member of the Stead team, was ready for his own show, too, in the Midwest. Hickam was an unusual man of many talents. He had mathematical skills, research know-how, language facility, and a good sense of humor along with its allied sense of broad perspective. As a child he had turned a negative situation into a positive one and profited with regard to patient needs from his own lengthy bout with osteomyelitis. He was a notable scholar when he was at Harvard and turned down an opportunity for a scholarship at the medical school there, in order to follow Stead south instead.

Dr. James Warren was an essential part of the team. His associate, Dr. McIntosh, referred to him as his immediate boss [with a little 'b'], but Stead was the 'Big Boss'. Dr. Warren embodied scientific curiosity. He was key in 'the Gator caper',

79

noted in chapter two. When he was denied an opportunity to study giraffes' blood pressures in Kenya, because of a dangerous uprising from the Maumau tribe, he stuck his neck out and found another locale in South Africa to investigate these beautiful creatures.

Another long-term colleague deserves further mention; Henry McIntosh, a war veteran who had previously attended the University of Pennsylvania Medical School. Henry had been a resident at Duke, as well, and he had been instrumental in running the cardiac catheterization laboratory. He traveled to Baylor many times and finally accepted the post of Chairman of Medicine there [see next chapter]. Although he was advised by Dr. Stead soon after his own retirement to shore up the 'free money', PDC-like clinic issue in Houston, analogous to that at Duke Medical Center, Henry accepted Dr. Micheal DeBakey's offer and doesn't regret that move to this day. Dr. Stead also warned him that higher salaries do not necessarily translate into adequate academic freedom; a freedom Stead valued more than rank or reimbursement; a freedom he felt was tied to personal happiness. Dr. McIntosh stresses there were no enticements of a big salary for him from Baylor; it was only slightly increased from his previous salary level.

Stead did not attempt to keep any loyal faculty members with the lure of bettering their salary, as well as their standing. That really was not part of his overall strategy. He encouraged housestaff and colleagues to grow and retain mobility in their career goals. In most cases he did not try to compete for a faculty member; he just wanted the members of the team to be effective, happy, and maintain vitality and creativity. When a faculty member, like McIntosh, moved on, hopefully, they left a good apprentice behind, even though they might take some supporting staff to their new environs. The advantage to this method was that even though Stead lost a mature faculty member, the trainee had years of prime development and productivity left ahead. Besides that, the younger trainee offered a new perspective and, at the same time the departed faculty member and boss could develop their own career at another institution.

Stead also went to Texas and laid low for several months, following his retirement, to assist the President of Baylor, Dr. Michael DeBakey, in stabilizing the medical school [see next chapter on bailing out Baylor]. Among other issues, some minor differences arose between DeBakey and McIntosh over the role of the coronary bypass operation; a subject near and dear to the surgeon's heart, so to speak. After seven years at Baylor, Dr. McIntosh settled in Lakeland, Florida. He continued medical practice and founded 'Heartbeat International', an organization that initiated the practice of providing cardiac pacemakers to third world countries through corporate contributions; he was a successful, upbeat, veteran member of Duke's old 'rhythm section' [see chapters 10 and 11].

Translation of Latin phrase: Judge a tree by its fruits, not its leaves.

Considering Challenges with Dr. Stead

4

Castling; **Building Institutions**
by Robert L. Bloomfield

> *One of the chief defects in our plan of education in this country is that we give too much attention to developing the memory and too little to developing the mind; we lay too much stress on acquiring knowledge and too little on the wise application of knowledge. [22] William J. Mayo*

helluo librorum

In the summer of 1969, the famous surgeon, Dr. Michael DeBakey invited Dr. Eugene Stead and, his wife, Evelyn, to come to Houston for several months to assist him in the task of improving the program at Baylor Medical School, which had been through many transformations and had been reformed under changing leadership. Also, in recent years Baylor had been moved from Dallas to Houston and was still affected by the transition. Stead's skill in medical education was a sought after ability nationwide even after his early retirement. Baylor took some of its new structure from Duke and some faculty members came from that institution to fill the ranks of the renewed Baylor.

Prior to this, Stead disseminated his brand of medical training through his student, housestaff, and colleague emissaries that traveled from Durham to other institutions to spread the scholarly style. In this instance, the blue-eyed chairman emeritus, himself was going to the West to show them there, how it was done; how the wild, wonderful Duke University Medical Center [DUMC] was won.

The actual building blocks of a renowned medical center are not the red bricks, the red clay or the sturdy steel girders; it's the living and usually breathing [barely] students and faculty. Nothing bettered the tensile strength of these architectural elements more than Stead's thinking ward rounds. These bedside-based problem-solving sessions were one of the trademarks of his university-building system. Through them, students of medicine in all stages of training were thrown together in a group to teach each other; revealing weaknesses that each pupil realized required individual practice; 'Sound off, one, two.... [march down the hall to the next bedside, march everyone!].'

This kind of thinking was different than book, lecture, and text or test learning. Before, in classes, memorization of facts was the main thing; now, rearrangement of many bits of clinical information into unique patterns to solve clinical problems was required.

Dr. Henry McIntosh from Duke, became Baylor's new chair for the Department of Medicine at about this same time and as part of his initial agreement to come, he and Stead had required that Baylor be closely associated with the teaching hospital, the Methodist. It was essential to have access to the Methodist for teaching students. The department chair for Medicine at Baylor had to have a corresponding position at the Methodist Hospital. This was an absolute requirement if McIntosh would come to lead. In Henry's term as the chairman, the Department of Medicine thrived in Houston; though Stead thought Henry should have waited six more months before taking the job to get a more firm commitment from the president, Dr. DeBakey. However, after twenty one visits to Houston to shore up the deal, Henry felt it was time to start.

When, similarly, Stead had arrived at Duke, he was confronted with an institution that needed building. It would always be compared with a medical center steeped in tradition; i.e. Harvard. At Duke and at Emory, there was less tradition and the absence of an established standard could be turned to a fresh leader's advantage.

Before the second world war, Dr. McIntosh asked his compatriots at Davidson College where they would recommend he attend medical school. The name 'Duke' did not come up except as a name of a 'country-clubish' medical school of little stature. After he returned from Europe, Duke was still considered a second rate institution. He had been parachuting in the war and had refused his medical school deferment from military service at the University of Pennsylvania. By 1949, when the war was over, Henry was looking for a straight medical internship; everything in Pennsylvania, by state regulation, was rotating. At that point, he was tired and dizzy from parachuting and he was looking for non-rotating internships. After Eugene Stead had renovated DUMC, it was considered by McIntosh's advisors to be an outstanding medical facility, especially in internal medicine. Henry found it so.

Besides filling all the battle stations in Houston, Stead had to bring other skills to the table at Texas. They were the clinical determinants from Durham, bullish, borrowed, bent, basted, barbecued and brought to Baylor:

1. Politics-Stead was a tempered, hard-ball politician; always over-prepared for committee meetings with administrators and other healthcare team members [e.g. nurses, nursing assistants, secretaries] He knew how to broker a deal where every party involved would benefit.
2. Delegating-He always was able to find a young faculty member to accept a position with certain clinical, teaching, or research responsibilities. He had a persuasive way to convince someone to pick up a new project and win battles.
3. Thinking Ahead-About 30 years before many others were praising computers, Stead envisioned multiple applications for diagnosis, management, and healthcare delivery, as well as economics for this burgeoning technology.
4. Combining Medical and Research Education-Faculty and students benefited from time to think and rearrange data. He knew one needed both kinds of development to build a

86

great university that could do things that others could not. In addition, he provided students with several role models for their future careers in medicine; researchers with some free time to teach and think, or clinicians dedicated to patient responsibilities, primarily, or some combination of these.

5. Separating Academic Rank and Salary-At DUMC, a faculty member could have lots of rank and little income or vice versa. Young doctors would have some reasonable rank and protected time to do what they wanted during their formative years. Money and academic work were dissociated and did not interfere with each other. This departmental flexibility allowed young faculty to accept opportunities elsewhere. Stead knew they would not stay forever, anyway. Of note, when Dr. McIntosh moved to Baylor, he was lured by academic goals, not by financial incentives.

Taking the Bypass Around Baylor

Drs. DeBakey and McIntosh got along splendidly; each supportive of the other. In addition, Dr. DeBakey was one of those 'Stead-like' types, McIntosh had been familiar with previously. Henry McIntosh met with DeBakey almost every morning about 7:00 for a clinical chat. A devoted Dr. DeBakey had frequently slept in his office the night before; his office had

"... adequate bathroom facilities", Dr. McIntosh recalls. By the mid '70s, the Chairman of Medicine became concerned about the large number of patients undergoing coronary artery bypass operations [CABGs]; McIntosh did not agree that as many of the patients should undergo the operation. While he did not express his concern immediately, he did publish his non-invasive views in the prestigious journal, *Circulation [9]* and expounded these opinions at an AHA session in Miami. To avoid further disagreements with Dr. DeBakey, which McIntosh felt might adversely affect the Department of Medicine that he had developed, this chair resigned without regrets. He moved to his native Florida to continue to provide clinical services for patients. The two physicians remain friends to this day.

As a lowly medical student at DUMC, I recall attending a lecture class with Dr. David Sabiston where that prominent surgeon expressed confidence that the indications for CABGs would widen and be supported by large, carefully conducted, scientific studies. That was 25 years ago. The indications have not broadened that greatly, though diagnosis, techniques and technology, anti-coagulation, medical treatment of arteriosclerosis, prevention, and less invasive measures have progressed substantially.

Dr. McIntosh's disclaimers are joined by the negative endorsement against too many CABGs from Dr. Bernard Lown, one of our contributors, a renowned cardiologist, a Nobel prize recipient, and author [34]. Dr. Stead also supports these cautions. To rephrase Dr. Paul Beeson's accolade at Dr. Stead's retirement symposium in consideration of this caution: [We should listen to all these able and caring 'greats']-"That would be to everyone's good fortune because [they are] great [men]."

An article of faith ... as indispensable is the Swan - Ganz line (a catheter inserted in the right side of the heart) for treating sick patients with heart failure. It has been in use for more than 25 years and is accepted as the gold standard for proper care. In the USA, this invasive technique is utilized in one million patients annually. Yet, only last year was the procedure subjected to a clinical evaluation which proved a bomb shell; it showed that its use was accompanied by a substantial mortality, a lengthened hospitalization and ballooned medical costs. While other procedures may not be as dangerous, nonetheless, few have been ... studied and most are used excessively. This is true for pacemakers, endoscopy, cesarean sections, fetal monitoring, etc.; procedures we all take for granted.

adapted from an article by Bernard Lown, M.D.
Jan., 2001   [see chapter 11 below]

Dr. Stead performed a great service to Baylor at a critical time and helped stabilize the situation here. His considerable academic experience and proficiency, his professional leadership, and his vision were valuable to a young school in establishing high standards of excellence and in recruiting highly qualified faculty members, especially from Duke. Dr. Stead's superb medical and scientific capabilities in education, his critical faculties, and his ability to inspire those who work with him are now legendary. I have the greatest esteem and affection for Eugene Stead, not only for his many contributions to medicine, but for his personal qualities and his ethics. Medicine owes him a great debt of gratitude.

Michael E. DeBakey, M.D., Professor of Surgery, Baylor College of Medicine Houston, Texas April, 2000   [7]

Lessons from Dealing with a Big League Team

As a team captain of Duke Medical, Stead learned a lot about coordinating a lot of different personalities and styles for an effective medical department. This is demonstrated well in his interactions with Dr. Kempner. Patients with difficult problems, like kidney or heart failure, would improve under Kempner's care and Stead would have to admit that Kempner was very capable and successful, though Stead and, also, the traditional scientific community couldn't exactly put their finger on why!!!? The role of sodium reduction in blood pressure control was not appreciated by other clinical researchers. Dr. Stead had actually gotten NIH money for Kempner against the Surgeon General's expert advise and an overruled committee of peers.

One might describe Walter Kempner as a bit 'stiff-necked'. He did not alter his patient management practices in all his years at Duke. Dr. McIntosh points out that even as new antihypertensive medications were developed and became available, Kempner continued to employ his same dietary approach, stressing weight reduction and sodium [salt] restriction. Many faculty and house-staff were critical of this perceived stubborn nature. Dr. Stead may have interpreted it as consistency. Kempner was invited to present some of his data to the New

York Academy of Sciences. Following his presentation, a prominent cardiologist criticised the findings, stating before the crowd, "... [you've- (referring to Kempner)] desecrated this great historic building [with] ... falsehood." Needless to say, Kempner never went back to a major scientific meeting again.

> *It should be appreciated that Dr. Kempner developed his program and demonstrated striking improvement in the control of severe hypertension and regression of the complications thereof when the only other therapy was phenobarbital. ...[W]ith the development of effective pharmacologic agents... Kempner shifted his effort to weight reduction. His reputation was so respected, that he attracted large numbers of ... patients from around the world. He managed ... patients in a ... "Rice House", [separate from] the Duke campus.*
>
> *Henry McIntosh, M.D.*

It's my opinion [not speaking for Dr. Stead], that there are some 'difficult people' pursuing medicine; ask my wife, she's married to one. However, one characteristic I lack, that Kempner had, is his gifted clinical style. Now, speaking for Dr. Stead, if Kempner had been a stereotypical physician, then there would never had been a Kempner program, a rice-diet, or any of his many other accomplishments. He had to be different. 'I come not to praise Kempner, but not to bury him either'. [Oh, by the way, could you pass the Caesar salad and the rice cakes, too, please??]

Duke afforded Stead freedom, as a department chairman, that allowed him to do things that team members did not necessarily approve of or like. That means that he could choose to develop the career of some 'fureigner that didn't quite fit in'.

91

Committee approval of a faculty member, in contrast, might derail a promising, creative track or career bound for discovery. 'Different' individuals, who varied from their peers; who were not considered 'normal', may have done some things foreign to the group norm. Stead never thought that the Department of Medicine ought to be like a country club. On the other hand, a department with a strong, vital leader had the flexibility to diversify and accept, absorb, and even develop 'different' kinds of doctors with various styles. The DUMC Department of Medicine had that kind of leader.

For those readers more interested in the details of Stead's unequaled administrative skills, which, by the way, he is quick to downplay, I suggest that they write me, Dr. McIntosh, Dr. Laszlo, Dr. Finn, Dr. B. Haynes or Dr. G.Wagner either via their respective universities, organizations or to be forwarded by this publisher. From these last mentioned, more experienced sources, I have ascertained some key rules in a nutshell for successful, and somewhat painless, administrating according to Stead [with less mid-cycle (that is, mid-fiscal-cycle) cramping]:

1. The Concept of 'Free Money': The size of the budget for the Department of Medicine at DUMC was not as big as some, but, according to Stead that did not tell the whole story. It really mattered most how much money the chairman could use that was uncommitted to salaries, buildings, and programs already [free money]. The PDC, especially, provided Stead with quite a bit of 'free money' with which he could purchase equipment or obtain potential faculty members; i.e. people of importance in his own, not necessarily in some committee's, estimation.

2. Eye Contact: There is swaying power and a sense of confidence and justice transmitted in one's visage. When ''ol daddy blue eyes' suggested something, you might not agree with it, but you were sure going to listen to his reasoning. His towering figure gently looked at you and impressed the listener. Whereas, with others one might view dollar signs in their dilating pupils, as the listener peered back into Dr. Stead's eyes, he or she would only see some nickels he had won in scholastic bets with residents.

3. Communicating in Person vs. by Memo: Visiting faculty members in person, even adversaries, provided an advantage in the art of negotiation. Meeting with people face-to-face, in contrast to communicating by memo, was more personal and denoted respect for the other individual. The subsequent interaction gave Stead a better bargaining atmosphere and led to important future contacts, even if he was not totally successful in a particular confrontation. Contrast this with a previous Dean at DUMC who communicated with faculty members through their spouses [for example, Evelyn Stead].

4. Manpower and Teamwork: Not only could Stead find a member of his team to accept a new project to oversee, his team bench was quite deep and included those in other departments. When Dr. McIntosh went to Baylor, he was accompanied by cooperative players from many sections-team players he could network with and delegate to. Similarly, when Dr. John Hickam went to the University of Indiana as Chief of Medicine, he took Dr. Stuart Bondurant to help. Stead explained, one person has too much to do at a new institution unless they bring others with them. Taking colleagues with you is also a means for judging the existence of 'free money'. If a new place can not offer additional funds to bring a supportive team member, that is probably an indication they don't usually have uncommitted money; and future negotiations may be troubled.

5. The Rule of Changes [Holding it Steady]: On the first day of his chief residency under Stead, Dr. Robert Whalen stated that Dr. Stead gave him the most useful advice for running a medical service: "Be careful, most people do not really want what they say they want; there will be a lot of people that will ask you to change things. In reality, they don't want these changes." The very same people who ask for changes are the same ones that will be most unhappy with them. So, be cautious about making big administrative changes in a working, existent program.

6. The Role of Private Patients: Veterans and charity patients in Stead's estimation, tended to be members of a 'captive audience', allowing medical students and young residents to apply what they had learned. While this was usually correct, Dr. Stead felt that there was an advantage to learning with patients who were less passive and prone to complain regarding clinical issues other than simple management [such as bedside manner, or personality].

94

7. Making Quick Decisions: Not only could Dr. Stead think, he could do it fast on his feet. He was never one, he exclaims, "to stew over a decision." While he noted that this characteristic guaranteed that he had little in the way of emotional investment in some issue, it also assumed that he could exercise good administrative judgement. The timer was clicking and he was making good moves before the alarm went off.

Building Resources

Texas is an expansive place; it feels as big as the entire southeastern U.S.; by car you can drive straight on a highway and not see a soul, city, or cellular phone tower for miles of flat, warm, grazing pastures. It is attractive to patients if an area offers the strengths in many subspecialties, as well as in general medicine and surgery. Stead had reinforced multiple resources on campus, including basic sciences like physiology and biochemistry; with their relationship to medicine. Off campus too, he had fortified resources. Many at Duke in the late '40s wanted their soon-to-be rival, the University of North Carolina, to be built farther away in Charlotte. Dr. Stead voted to have it closer to Durham, in Chapel Hill. Down the road, it could bolster those weaker resources at Duke and serve as a potential site for collaborations and spousal employment. In addition, there was Research Triangle Park, which served as a similar resource.

In Boston, Philadelphia, Baltimore and New York City, there was a concentration of medical, science, and social science talents, as well as great universities; oases of scholarship packed in a virtual, but densely populated desert. The Southeast and Texas needed that density of skills in certain regions and they had more room to grow. Duke had gone places in the eyes of the medical and scientific community and Baylor would, too.

A Very Brief and Partial History of Baylor and Houston

Houston is a grand city and the community leaders had a big part in its success, which has resulted in the Methodist Hospital, M. D. Anderson Hospital, the Children's Hospital, Ben Taub Public Hospital and the Texas Medical Center. Dedicated 'Houstonians' financed the construction of a ship channel nearly 50 miles long; because a great city should have access to the ocean. A great city should also have a fine medical school. So, in 1943, they financed the transfer of Baylor College of Medicine from Dallas to Houston, initially, located in a renovated, vacant Sears Roebuck warehouse. Then, in 1948, they lured the heart surgeon, Dr. Michael Debakey, from Louisiana. Those Texans had a natural knack for mobilizing resources. Back in the mid 1930s, though banks were failing all over the country, the city leaders made sure the great city of Houston's banks stayed solvent during the Depression. When things got bumpy in the late '60s with regard to medical education, Drs. Stead, McIntosh, and some other 'Durhamites' touched down in Texas; some of McIntosh's patients flew to Baylor to see him when he shuttled west to direct the Medicine Department. 'Houston, we have a problem, but we'll deal with it.'

Preparation for Practice

Each medical center will have its individual flavor that complements the surrounding environment. Many students and established practitioners maintain the misconception that interns and residents need to be exposed to every clinical situation they will ever be confronted with in practice. That's impossible, and Stead believed in maximizing limited resources in the desert around the medical oasis. Like Dr. Stead, we should water and nurture the growing students, who, in turn, will irrigate, rather than irritate, the community doctors with knowledge and language transmitting the medicine of tomorrow, as well as the latest, cutting edge medicine of today. The established physicians would, in turn, teach the young doctors useful information regarding the current medical practice of today; much of it, non-medical.

Practice is a lifelong pursuit, which Dr. Stead believed should be filled with continuing education. In practice, one takes care of well and sick patients and hospital experiences do not necessarily prepare you for years of 'accepting new patients' of every variety. In keeping with his approach to medical edification, Stead held that good doctors were "made by practice, not by training." He wanted to produce practitioners that would actively participate in applying what they learned about medicine, not only in teaching it.

Medicine, practiced in the community, is always in a state of flux. Even the types of practices [for example, preventive] are changing. The secret to a successful medical career, in Stead's estimation, was to devise a training program that was flexible and could absorb changes. Both faculty members and students in medical universities will grow. Exactly how they will grow is uncertain. Yet, for most faculty, Stead noticed over the years, that their productivity in medicine diminished. He believed that to remain vital, the young should carry the torch and the older physicians should move into other, sometimes cooler and shadier, areas of university or community responsibility.

Specialists vs. Generalists

In *A Way of Thinking [16]*, compiled essays of Dr. Stead's, by Dr. Barton Haynes, Stead suggests residents in general internal medicine read *The Second World War* by Churchill. He considered Winston Churchill to be similar to a fine generalist who surrounded himself with gifted specialists. Churchill integrated all the information given to him by various commanders, but always remained in charge, directing operations.

Stead's point was that the generalist must depend on skillful specialists, but he or she must stay in charge and direct others to carry out their health strategies. This requires that the generalist has a strong ego and that he or she enjoys taking charge. It also requires constant updating one's knowledge, because the general health field is very wide indeed. Besides being knowledgeable in the area of health and disease, the general physician must hone his people skills; his bedside or 'tableside' or 'chairside' or 'phoneside' manner. The generalist is more dependent on non-medical subjects [such as, history, social sciences, cultures] than the specialist.

I am not saying that the generalist is more 'cultured' than the specialist; just that the generalists depends on humanities and other subjects; more so than the specialists for their livelihood. While we are on the subject of cultures, let's digress a little to show that this distinction is quite evident in the way we approach common infectious diseases. As Stead points out in the book by Dr. Haynes, the hospital-based infectious disease specialist treats really sick, often immuno-compromised patients. These patients are infected with resistant organisms, already exposed to other antibiotics; they often have many associated, complicating illnesses and several essential medications. Testing has been done for suspected 'bugs' and sensitivities are routinely accomplished in a hospital laboratory. Other procedures not always available in the community can be done quickly, backed up by a staff of experts. Contrast this with 'local medical docs' [LMDs] who are confronted with a different set of needs; patient requirements which may include compliance problems, family issues, transportation difficulties, economic shortfalls, besides circumstances beyond their control; in the community, the choice of antibiotic and the duration of treatment may be quite different. Preceding this description, the 'raconteur', Dr. Stead, quotes the old adage, "Where you stand determines what you see." Churchill spent much of his time on an island; a different and relevant perspective was provided from allies on the mainland.

A Note From Dr. McIntosh

Dr. Stead taught Dr. McIntosh some important lessons about patient care. He's not sure where he learned the following quote from, but he is quite sure that Dr. Stead believes it:

> *If you plan for a year, plant rice;*
> *If you plan for 10 years, plant trees;*
> *If you plan for 100 years, educate men.*
> *Confucius*

Thus, Dr. McIntosh has tried to teach one person something new and useful each day. Henry McIntosh also quotes a statement from the late, great cardiologist, Paul Dudley White, for whom Stead had much admiration:

> *...trivial remarks, actions ... may destroy the confidence*
> *... of the patient and ... prevent evolution of the case.*
> *...at the ... outset ... the physician must use the greatest*
> *care.*
> *P. D. White*

He has reflected on the lessons Dr. Stead has taught him and developed **The Ten Commandments of Patient Care**:

1. Thou shalt always give the patient the feeling that you have time for him/her.
2. Thou shalt always listen to and observe the patient.
3. Thou shalt always be concerned about all of the patient's symptoms and seek the cause or explanation of each.
4. Thou shalt always, at each visit, review the patient's current medications and look for side effects.
5. Thou shalt always seek to educate the patient as to the cause of symptoms.
6. Thou shalt always try to prevent chronic disease and/or disability.
7. Thou shalt always, when recommending a new therapy or study for the patient, ask-"Should I?"
8. Thou shalt always, when functioning as a consultant, remember that you are the consultant to the patient and not to the referring physician.
9. Thou shalt always be totally honest with the patient.
10. Thou shalt always be concerned about the cost of care to the patient and the society at large.

(For a patients' Bill of Rights, the inquisitive readers are referred to their local representatives)

An Additional Note About Teamwork

Teamwork was an essential element in many parts of the program that Stead promoted. One function it served in training young physicians was that it allowed inexperienced practitioners to get a chance to do or order procedures and direct the care of patients. Learning was best accomplished by being in charge of patient care and accepting responsibility. Success for the entire team was defined as taking care of people well. A good leader was needed by each healthcare team; and Stead trained good leaders.

Young physicians, as well as students, were assisted in their individual development by building on their different strengths. To paraphrase Dr. Stead, his goal was not to produce doctors from a 'common mold', but to identify the optimal use of a person's talents. In Stead's training program, the faculty would make the best use of the trainee, depending on the limits imposed by his or her particular makeup. Each student of medicine would gain satisfaction in clinical matters by a different approach. As Stead said, "... [W]e honored the [doctor] who did excellent general practice as much as the specialist, research scientist, and doctor with administrative talents." [26]

from What This Patient Needs is a Doctor, p32.

Translation of Latin phrase: A devourer of books.

5

Moving Pieces; **The Mind of Medicine**
by Robert L. Bloomfield

There is a side to human behavior in health and disease which is not a thing of intellect, which is irrational and emotional but important. It is the mainspring of most of what we do and a great deal of what we think. It is being explored by psychiatry but it is in danger of being neglected by clinical science. [22] Sir Robert Platt.

labor ipse voluptas

During all his clinical experience as a medical student, psychiatry was the one rotation Stead didn't like; he wasn't alone in this regard. However, when he arrived at Duke as chairman, he found psychiatry a useful discipline to help in the care of his patients. Dr. Leslie Holleman taught Stead and shored up the new chairman's sense of inadequacy and in the process, they formed a lasting friendship. Moreover, the two agreed on the philosophy of behavior. Both physicians felt that the brain structure determines demonstrated behavior and both believed you couldn't change the brain all that much.

103

Behavior, in their views, had a neurological basis. Actually, in earlier years, Stead's work on the autonomic nervous system with his mentor, Soma Weiss, had suggested that there may be a structural component to psychiatric disorders. With all this in mind, Drs. Stead and Holleman both concentrated on people for whom one could accomplish some good and avoided spending a lot of time on those who they believed could not be helped. This concept concerning the structure of neurons [brain cells] had a relation to broadening the satisfying life experiences for physicians, as well as patients.

In the past, Stead had been a staunch supporter regarding the role of psychiatry in training and medical management. Back in Boston, during the war, Dr. Stead had worked with a psychiatrist, John Romano, who worked with and was influenced by George Engel [Frank's twin; see chapter 2]. Romano was able to address a lot of the problems that Stead could not fathom. All three doctors believed in understanding the patient's entire background, forming long-term relationships with them, being sensitive to the psycho-social aspects of medicine, and treating the 'whole' patient.

Dedication to Psychiatry/Psychology in Patient Care

One devoted chief resident, later to become a cardiology specialist, Dr. Robert Whalen, recalls that the medical team used to 'hide' so-called, 'psychosomatic' patients from the attention of Dr. Stead on ward rounds. This was done to avoid his time-consuming bedside pursuit of the search for more traditional, organically-definable disease to explain the 'crocky' complaints. Whalen remembers that these Stead symptom searches were so long that residents feared that these prolonged interviews might give rise to varicose veins in their own lower limbs from 'bedside teaching standstill'. Stead would not allow residents to employ the term, 'crock', no matter how absurd the patient complaint seemed ["Doc, my teeth itch and my skin has this creepy feeling"]. Unfathomable complaints from patients were seen as means individuals were using to cope with stresses in the environment. Many of these patients would benefit from being examined by a psychiatrist, but not always for the conventional reasons most people conceive of.

Chief residents at Duke were also all enrolled in psychoanalysis sessions as part of their training. Why? Not because they required it medically, although some say anyone who would accept that kind of discipline as a medical resident needs to have their head examined. Stead, however, felt that the house officers with the greatest responsibility would be more productive and happier with this psychotherapy. Some of the residents became very depressed and unable to do the large workload entrusted to them. So, each week, the chief resident would have a session to explore personal 'issues' with Dr. Bingham Dai, a psychologist of Asian descent at Duke hospital. There was the hope that busy residents would find inner peace [om, om my goodness]. According to Dr. McIntosh, participating residents acted, at times, like they were being forced into dialysis, rather than simply psychoanalysis. This was just one aspect of Stead's program that was truly unique.

This notion of productivity in the medical workplace being harmed by hostility or dissatisfaction impacted Stead's teaching rounds and his directing of 'morning report'. He would bring up these attitudinal issues on the wards, at the nursing stations, and at the breakfast table. Each locale served as a forum to express his concepts of the fulfilled healthcare provider.

Dr. Whalen also recalls that Dr. Stead had an unusual way of looking at staff, students, and clinical problems; but, at the same time, he was analyzing extra data that residents were not even considering in formulating the long-term plan for the patient. For example, the family structure and the environment were important considerations. Dr. Myers, a close associate, recalls, while one did not understand how he came to his conclusions, and though his ideas seemed a bit unconventional, in spite of everything, Stead was usually right. His views about patient care and medical training were related; and understanding behavior and feeling or intuition played an important role in each.

Human Qualities and Homunculi

Stead believed, even before it was common knowledge, that the brain was somewhat changeable, though major changes might require a lot of input of time and energy by the practitioner. He felt this plasticity of the central nervous system [CNS] was more characteristic in the human embryo and the young child. As the brain got older, it became less malleable. I often reminisce about several things I could have done myself, but did not, because I was trying to conserve brain cells; I probably could have done them when I had a reserve of young, healthy neurons; it's much too late now [hey, maybe not!]. The complicated network of neurons in the CNS appears to develop in response to repetitive input from the environment. The peripheral nerves in contact with the surroundings have a somewhat proportional representation of all the body parts in the brain; the 'homunculus'. There exists a little person represented in the sensory or motor strips of the cerebral cortex [right under the top of our skulls].

In the child, this and other neurologic manifestations of the 'real world' may not be fully formed and may be subject to outside stimuli to change. Stead believed that this nerve-structural change could be accompanied by a positive change in behavior. Thus, children's brains, he feels, is a very precious resource indeed; the care of children, the instruction of the young, and the prevention of catastrophic illness is one of the most important responsibilities of any society.

By the time a person has aced all the tests [premed and med and non-med], jumped all the hurdles, and formed their attitudes toward learning and the like, the brain has developed, in Stead's view, almost irreversible changes. These changes relate to religious beliefs, fears, fantasies, personal habits, as well as attitudes toward parents, peers, paternal, and maternal figures. By the time this person entered medical school, Dr. Stead observed that these irreversible changes resulted in learning limitations that dominated the training period. Psychoanalysis, within certain margins, could optimize performance of the student; but, it couldn't easily raise the ceiling of the brain's limitations without the expenditure of an inordinate amount of energy by the teacher and individual student.

Structure and Function

Soma Weiss and Eugene Stead were both aware of the essential role of the nervous system in determining and altering behavior of the cardiovascular system. Since the '40s, concepts of how structure affects functions have changed. Our vision of the elements which lead to functioning has become more acute; more focused and more microscopic. We now have newer tools to view physiologic changes; electron microscopes, fluorescent microscopes, isotopes, antibodies, and antigens for labeling. We are now more conscious of circulating substances, membrane structures, receptors, enzymes, lipids, and genes. Learning and defining anatomy has altered our understanding of the correlate, 'function'.

Stead found the concept of 'functional' illness unacceptable and merely a manifestation of our own ignorance; he considered it anathema on ward rounds. Woe to the student who explained a patient's chief complaint on the basis of so-called 'functional' [non-organic] disease. In addition, the specialist was not immune from Stead's criticism either. The Chairman of Medicine felt that cardiologists needed to "look beyond the heart" in evaluating a problem; and, in the same respect, the neurologist needs to think beyond and in greater depth about the myelin sheath and other anatomic structures he or she can relate to in their therapeutic approach. In <u>A Way of Thinking</u> by Dr. B. Haynes [16], Stead quotes the neurologist, MacDonald Critchley: "Is this a psychiatric affection ...? I submit that it is not; but an organic affection of obscure origin."

Thus, both the psychiatrist and the generalist, who direct healthcare for their patient over many years in multiple situations, may be in touch with basic disorders that affect the functioning of the human organism in the 'real world'. They both are not as likely as the specialists to tell the patient or practitioner, "This is not a heart [or nerve] problem [something I was taught about in med school]; you really don't need to consult me!" At times, the specialists only attend to what they understand from medical textbooks or related literature in their chosen fields of practice. The specialist is, however, more likely to recognize an unusual malady and less likely to say to the patient, "Take two aspirin and call me in the morning."

So, who should teach the trainees the essentials about the relationship between structure and function in medical school? Stead believed that the faculty in the departments of Medicine, Pathology, Biochemistry, Pharmacology, Physiology and Anatomy would provide the necessary faculty. To get more satisfaction from the practice of medicine, the medical student was asked to learn more about the patient that had the disease; the actual person with the disorder, not just about the homunculus.

Bringing it Home [even for homely homunculi]

Most medical students are quite intelligent and you can quote me on that. I.Q.s, S.A.T.s, M.C.A.T.s and many other measures of cerebral prowess for this subgroup raises many an eyebrow on university admissions committees. However, the I.Q. portion of the brain is a limited segment of the grey matter. Dr. Stead always described himself not as examination-sensitive, but as performance-sensitive, instead. Brains, and their attached bodies dangling below, were limited most by other portions of the cerebral cortex that contained neurons arranged for certain behaviors. To be a 'Steadman' [not a brain-deadman] team member, one's sub- and supratentorial [brainy] assets had to outweigh one's liabilities [for example, a bad attitude]. One had to be able to keep up on bedside rounds: so-called, 'Steadman Walking' rounds. Still, there would always be arenas in which those liabilities would be prominent and a high level of productivity was lacking. No individual was expected to do it all.

The team smoothed over some of these inadequacies; I mean, no body's perfect, right? Stead's own inadequacies were covered up by other team members. Stead recalls being at the 1981 Kentucky Derby and happily discovering that his long history of 'malamusicism' [tune/tone deafness] had suddenly improved. Unfortunately, as his wife, Evelyn, pointed out, the audience was standing for *The Star Spangled Banner*, not for *My*

110

Old Kentucky Home; the tune he thought, mistakenly, that he was hearing. Everyone has their limits.

Bringing people of diverse talents together under the roof of one institution leads to important collaborations and remarkable discoveries. Stead did that a great deal at Harvard, Emory, and Duke. Remember Bill Castle from The Thorndike in Boston [see chapter 2]? He got together with Linus Pauling and they worked out that electrophoresis could separate the hemoglobin from sickle cell anemic patients distinct from normal hemoglobin. This led to defining the molecular structure of this abnormal blood cell protein and, ultimately, to improving management of a difficult disorder. In most instances of diagnoses, we have determined the abnormal function, classified it and named it long before we have identified the structural changes, be they micro- or macroscopic, that actually explain the underlying cause for that dysfunction.

Abnormal function of the well-protected organ, the brain, has been described, studied classified, and reclassified **non-invasively** by psychiatrists, psychologists, and neurologists. Stead has credited psychoanalysts with two important contributions to our understanding of brain function. According to Dr. Stead, these 'head hunters' have clearly demonstrated that brain structure is due to the combined effect of genetic and environmental influences. These have their greatest effects before birth and during infancy. Psychoanalysts have also shown us how hard it is to change brain structure by merely talking. One might conclude from this that support groups related to healthcare should complement their group sessions with appropriate activities. Stead would 'talk the talk' but, he would also 'walk the walk'.

The Good, the Bad, the Sick, the Well, and the Ugly

Not only could the environment change the brain structure, but, Stead felt that the brain would lose organic substance from disuse. Yet, even with so-called 'normal' brain substances, there was a wide range of functional variability. An individual may have had a high I.Q., but be dyslexic. A great medical scholar may have been slightly uncoordinated and continually bumping his head on door frames in front of ward or board rooms. Thus, various minor 'abnormalities' may exist in an otherwise normal brain. These variations are often overlooked in the routine physical examination. Still, these differences are significant when managing medical problems and predicting how patients will compensate for their disorders.

Given a choice, Stead always preferred caring for the person who was basically well, as opposed to extremely sick patients. Those with serious diseases carried two sets of problems; all the difficulties belonging to well individuals plus, problems created by the illness. Many of Dr. Stead's associates preferred to care for severely ill patients; those in which disease dominated the clinical presentation. In these latter cases, the subtle differences in CNS structure are overshadowed by the acute illness. In this situation the practitioner, not the patient, is

112

the party responsible for compensating; making the environment 'disease-friendly'.

When the medical crisis subsides, the quirks of brain structure and function become more obvious. These quirks may be manifested as behavioral shortcomings which can be "corrected" by another "more average person", to quote Dr. Stead. In my opinion, these so-called quirks or "disabilities", as Stead refers to them, may offer a new, fresh perspective. Crossed eyes may require corrective surgery, but, in the meantime, compensation for visual problems may lead to seeing what others with 'normal' eyes can not, like in those popular, 3-D appearing, 'magic eye' pictures. The compensation may not seem immediately useful at the time, but undetermined changes in brain structure may provide an unforeseen advantage. Whether you are an extremely uncustomary man like Dr. Kempner, a mental giant; like the examining men–Drs. Hickam and Engel, or a mutant like one of the X men, quirks of brain structure may give you an unusual power. That power might make you a sought after member of some special society or to be drafted by some unusual healthcare team.

Dr. Stead believed that brains of differing structures could also be sorted into different categories, depending on their strengths or weaknesses. However, he did not discriminate in other general ways. Unlike his colleagues, he found 'brain sorting' a fascinating and a useful concept in clinical practice. It probably helped him in his long-term management of patients and in his constant 'talent scouting' for potential 'Stead team' members.

113

Daily Satisfactions While Developing a Career in Medicine

Garnering rewards from daily interactions with patients was at the base of the Stead methods of training. These emotional rewards were then shared with the healthcare team. Dr. Stead found that in this process of sharing, the clinician became an effective recruiter and trainer [Training and use of paramedical personnel, *NEJM*, 277: 800, '67; (17)]. In that same article, Stead lists the extensive healthcare team; everyone from the receptionist, through the nurse's aid, to the "narrowly active specialist."

These medical and paramedical personnel improve the responsiveness of the healthcare team, particularly by allowing the sick, often irrational, patient to make demands without incurring resentment from the team. Some of these non-physician personnel may be career-minded, but the flexibility of the team approach allows some less career-minded individuals to enter and exit the field.

Had the social and economic structure been different, some of these ancillary healthcare people might have become doctors. Since, both universities and governing bodies have resources to direct healthcare, it was Stead's contention that they had the responsibility to experiment and mix existing health professionals in unique combinations to provide better health delivery for all. New forms of healthcare providers needed to be developed; thus the Physician Assistant programs were born ["It's alive!; and it's still alive and well].

The lot of the medical students needed improvements as well. The training of the physician was rife with delayed gratification; filled with so many years of preparation. Sacrifice of most things, sprinkled with an occasional vacation or golf game, was par for the course. If the young doctor was considering a program or a position in which satisfaction was dependent on achieving some distant goal, Dr. Stead would advise against it. However, if there was much satisfaction to be gained as one progressed up the hierarchy and the trainee enjoyed the process, then one could not lose. The educational track of the young doctor ought to teach him or her to enjoy the patients they were caring for.

As a doctor moved out into practice, patients actually became part of that educational process. In Dr. Stead's words as a practicing physician, he'd say to the patient: "I'm going to give you the best service over the years, but that requires that I continue my education," He then proposed that community physicians set aside one day each week to see patients free of charge as part of continuing education, without attention to office overhead or other distractions. By separating income from clinical activities, Stead felt that these activities were accomplished primarily for continuing medical education. By staying active in medical education and seeing some patients for learning, rather than for production, the practitioner would beat the dreaded 'forgetting curve'.

Seeking Fame and, Instead, Getting Four Chins in the Process of Pursuing a Medical Career

Have you ever looked back at the paper trail of medical literature to see if you can find those scientists or doctors that first described something during their academic careers punctuated by the requirement to 'publish or perish'. They published all right, but Stead discovered they perished, as well. He has looked up the discoverers of vitamin B12 and the describers of pernicious anemia, Drs. Minot and Murphy. Their two names no longer appear in the standard textbooks of medicine; no longer does Stead's name, or his team members' names appear [you know, the et. al.s in all those publications] to give them credit for their work, either. Even if they were listed at the end of a scientific article, they might go unnoticed or given as much attention as the credits that role by at the end of a foreign film.

Discoveries from the laboratories provided by Dr. Stead or his colleagues may have been discovered by a lot of people before, but, somehow, that knowledge remained hidden or unapplied. Stead and company would laugh at their own presumptions and pride that they were viewed as the explorers when they found out afterward that some other thinkers had beaten them to the truth.

Let's stop fooling ourselves; Dr. Stead did. No matter how great you become, your discoveries, your publications, your theories, won't last all that long. Even syndromes or orifices with

116

your name attached to them may get changed someday; so sorry, 'doc'.

> *you can read the ... papers ... but how do you divine what the human spirit has contributed to a profession or society.*
>
> *Robert Whalen, M.D., former chief resident and Professor of Medicine, Division of Cardiology; DUMC From J. Laszlo, M.D. [unpublished manuscript] [28]*

Dr. Whalen recounts a story in John Laszlo's manuscript comparing the differing styles regarding publications between Eugene Stead and Dr. Eugene Braunwald, previous Chairman of Medicine at Harvard and Chief of Cardiology. The latter had over 450 articles attributed to him in his bibliography. Braunwald was known for his prodigious writing and rewriting many papers from associates that he stimulated. However, he did come under scrutiny when a co-writer, Darsee, published some fraudulent research. While no one can criticize Dr. Braunwald for having his name on those papers, Dr. Stead would not attach his name to anything that he did not actively participate in, even the research that he stimulated. Stead wouldn't even allow others to acknowledge him at the end of a paper for submission. If anything came out of his department, he would check its authenticity meticulously. An associate in the Department of Medicine would have to defend a proposed article, like a thesis, in front of Stead before it was submitted for publication. Whalen recalls, "Compared to Stead, peer review was nothing ... if we could get it past [him], we could get it past any editorial board." Getting the present text past him also required several reviews; and he didn't feel his name should be attached [editor's note].

Stead was also on several editorial boards himself. Back in his early career at Emory, he had been introduced to <u>The Classics of Medicine Library</u> by one of his associates. He'd always been a lover of books, so the leather binding was a good fit for him. After his early retirement, he edited the journal, *Circulation* and the more regional publication, *The North Carolina Medical Journal*. [see chapter 7]

One could think of Eugene Stead as an accomplished explorer, as talented as Jacque Cousteau. Dr. Stead was a charismatic, deeply gifted leader; he helped open up a new world for all of us to see. Stead's view of the world was not pressurized underwater, but remained near sea level with the occasional hyperbaric oxygen. Eugene Stead, like Jacque Cousteau, attracted and immersed himself in productive people in a private, protected, and partially-explored place. The 'Stead Team', like the 'Cousteau Team', could accomplish more than any single individual could; and the team members received deserved credit for their patient work. Stead was perpetually curious about viewing old and uncharted environments through eyes provided by young, developing technologies. These environments, buried deep in the body, were filled with invaluable treasures. Although medical tides have shifted and the sea level has risen, the piers keep floating; Dr.

Stead has contributed a lasting *modus operandi* for fathoming medical problems.

For Eugene Stead, the means for solving clinical conundrums involved creating and modifying liaisons with practitioners and other team players. These collaborative bonds were quite flexible, like the bonds between two helical strands of DNA. In the laboratory, the sea sponge, the flatworm, and the hydra can all regenerate themselves after being forced through a wire mesh, using the basic genetic building-block information alone. Similarly, wherever Stead's students relocated, cohesive units and departments would reassemble, belying the years of teaching efforts it took to fuse them together; these units were modeled after complex genetic material-the stuff that people are made of.

A chosen few were picked to enter the Duke process of training. Even fewer accepted the demanding experience. This did not daunt the blue-eyed general, whom Dr. Whalen refers to as the "benign dictator". The cream of the crop, by academic standards, did not always want to subject themselves to the grueling schedule of the Department of Medicine at DUMC; and if you wanted to catch up on some extra sleep in the hospital, you had to hide in order to delay your involvement in emergent patient problems.

Dr. Stead did not value paper scores and awards as much as he valued devotion to medicine and a willingness to do hard work. If Dr. Stead met you and pierced you with his steely stare, he could scan you and tell what sort of a resident you would be. I mean, really, aren't the applicants within the top tiers pretty good anyway. So, we should bless the housestaff; in particular, the chief residents, as well as Dr. Stead, for the sacrifices they made to accomplish so much that has changed the way we practice medicine today. Listed below are the chief residents that did in years past what we hope others will continue to do:

> *The chief residency was, in a sense, a three-year tour of duty.*
> *Robert Whalen, M.D., former chief resident*

Chief Residents:

Samuel P. Martin 1947
Bernard C. Holland 1948
James F. Schieve 1949
Grace P. Kerby 1950
James W. Hollingsworth 1951
Gerald Rodnan 1952
Harry McPherson 1953
Morton Bogdonoff 1954
Suydam Osterhout 1955
Donald Merritt 1956
John V. Verner 1957
Arnold M. Weissler 1958
Robert E. Whalen 1959
Howard K. Thompson 1960
Charles E. Mengel 1961
T. David Elder 1962
Andrew G. Wallace 1963
Michael E. McLeod 1964
Earl N. Metz 1965
Harry M. Carpenter 1966

Translation of Latin phrase: Work itself is pleasure.

6

Why is this knight different from all other....; **Time to Think**
by Robert L. Bloomfield

You will have to learn many tedious things... which you will forget the moment you have passed your final examination, but in anatomy it is better to have learned and lost, than never to have learned at all. [22]   W. Somerset Maughham.

medicus curat, natura sanat

"...the personality of the artist or scientist...determines the ultimate character of the work. Therefore,..., the personality of the artist or scientist must be an essential element of study. The historian can do this by recording the impact of a person...by tracing...his lifetime. Without the human element, history becomes a recitation...of facts. This is even more true with medical science, which has as its final goal the application of science to human beings. The goals of the physician are primarily humanistic".

Richard J. Bing, M.D., in *The Evolution of the Science and the Art   [23]*

litterae sine moribus vanae   [see index]

A Passage for Posterity

(A poetic interlude for our readers)

What an honor it must be
To have a tube named after you,
Like our old friends Fallopius and Eustachius do,
So that passing on, you leave behind something that stuff can
keep on passing through.

Access for aqueous
Resides in the canal of Schlemm,
and Wharton has a duct that serves the flow of phlegm.
I get a lump in my sinus of Morgagni
When I sit and think of them.

For me, even part of a tube would do,
Like the ampulla of Abraham Vater,
Or the loops of Friedrich Gustav Jacob
Henle that carries so much water,
Or just some little niche
That some holy fellow hasn't already though' a'.

The entrance or exit
To an anatomic tunnel would suffice,
Like the sphincter of Oddi or a
Sphincter not quite as nice.

That odious egress upon which all beings human deign to sit.
I've so often been called the same, perhaps I was named after it!

by Robert L. Bloomfield, M.D., M.S.   [25]

Symposium for Stead

When Dr. Stead stepped down from the chairmanship at Duke, his colleagues were very disappointed. Few of his peers took him seriously when he had previously warned them that he intended to retire before his 60th birthday. When the reality occurred, they organized an appropriate send off by having a conference and published symposium in *The Annals of Internal Medicine* in November, 1968 [vol. 69, no. 5; (6)]. The tributes came from very distinguished attendees, but a less vocal tribute can be noted by the casual reader, as well. If one peruses the medical literature at that time from any prestigious journal, one would find that many of the articles come from Durham or institutions where Stead's friends reigned; Ohio, Indianapolis, Pittsburgh, and Atlanta.

The presentations at the symposium concentrated on CHF, vascular disease, and health service delivery. After the symposium, Dr. Stead moved to New York City, in part, to give room to the subsequent chairman, Dr. Jim Wyngaarden. He relinquished his position, but also made himself scarce, because his power was quite pervasive and the new chairman benefited somewhat from that absence, so he could mobilize and organize his own departmental resources. No longer would the phrase, "Gene's Department" be employed.

At that symposium, his long-time compatriot, Dr. John Hickam started the presentations with an introductory appreciation of Dr. Stead. In his address, he attempted to

123

enumerate the qualities that made Stead so charismatic; "critical, ambitious, competitive, ...competent, ...imaginative, ...hardworking...."; magnetic characteristics that brought so many scholars from the Brigham and Grady Hospitals years previously. Hickam went on to describe a comic strip character from mid-century, "Influence", that somehow captured the essence of those undefined qualities that Stead possessed. The search for those special, intangible characteristics proceed in Dr. Hickam's address; "...independent, ...skilled, ...ability to analyze a complicated problem, ...express...with clarity, ...a gift for colorful language, ...devotion...." The elusive answer may never be known, but may be approximated by two points made at the end of his friend's speech.

The first is that Stead was able, and expected his students to be able, to take in and absorb masses of data. From that data processing, he then expected the fine clinician or investigator to distill this information and formulate questions which would clarify a particular problem. The second point was that Stead's teaching, while universal, was directed toward the unselfish purpose of maximizing an individual student's growth. He "...helped [them] to understand, to grow, and to do what [they] can do."

Payment of the Infantrymen and the Healthcare Troops

In the 1930s and '40s, the salaries for the interns were in the single or double digits per year. Why, in those early days, it was very rare for a resident to be married. Young doctors ate, slept, and did their laundry at the hospital; they didn't walk miles without shoes in the snow to the hospital; the hospital was their home where, occasionally, they removed their shoes. They viewed snowfalls from inside the wards.

Dr. Stead had always been an advocate for better salaries for housestaff. Yet, as a chairman, he understood that even advanced residents might not generate all the income they required to make use of the medical facilities needed to learn their job. Still, their pay should, at least, allow them to minimize their accumulated debt from this prolonged training. He did not want concerns about monetary stability to create excessive pressure regarding a career decision. Whatever reimbursement was decided upon, Stead stressed, however, that the faculty must be entrusted by trainees with directing their education, with its underlying philosophy. This was based on the assumption that the troops of trainees had an intelligent, charismatic, and caring 'general'. Dr. Stead was such a leader.

In 1979, *The Annals of Internal Medicine [AIM]* published an article by Stead on medical education [19]. He reinforced his theme concerning the need to expand and mobilize our national health care troops. In this article, he reiterates that the primary product of medical schools is manpower; persons armed with new or burgeoning knowledge. Once the goal is shifted to production output and seeing the greatest number of patients economically, to balance the budget, this short-sighted, but fiscally-sound, goal spells failure for the educational aspect of the medical center. This represents a managed care directive that may be doomed to failure. Stead implores us to not reduce support for 'free' faculty teaching time.

Good clinical teachers are effective at imparting two types of medical information: that which is established practice [current information], the medicine of today, and that which is not yet known [research information], the medicine of tomorrow. With all the choices and a crowded curriculum, how can the student or resident create time to think and learn to manipulate so much data? There is so much to juggle and so little time. Enter the 'top sergeant' for the troops–the physician's assistant.

The Beginning of the PA Program

The story of Stead's development of the first PA program, a program that is a source of pride for Dr. Stead, starts first with the nursing staff at Duke hospital. Stead made several attempts to make nurses a part of his health care team and tried to help them reap financial benefits of participating in patient care. For one reason or another these attempts did not work out; either the hospital or the nurses themselves did not support the strategy. Making nurses so integral to health care management was unheard of previously.

Dr. Stead needed someone on the team who was ready to learn new skills, willing to accept clinical decision-making responsibilities; someone not already bogged down with clinical work; someone committed to devoting their life to the pursuit of

126

current medical knowledge; someone who was carefully assertive. Then, this 'sergeant' would report to the commander [the doctor], who now had time to stay current and give orders, in turn, to the supporting staff. The P. A. allowed the physician to be more effective. The physician would consider the recommendations of the sergeant, but the commander would make the final decision. Stead first employed firemen, then army corpsmen, and finally, students. His colleague, Henry McIntosh, actually did a lot of the ground work. He was developing the cardiac catheterization laboratory at Duke at that time and required personnel in the presence of a perpetual nursing shortage. Henry combed the yellow pages in the phone book to locate those that were used to emergency or urgency schedules and weren't apt to sleep on the job. When *Look Magazine* ran a story, published right after the first PAs graduated, the headline read: "Less Than a Doctor, Better Than a Nurse". Obviously, this offended the nurses and the medical faculty moved to a diplomatic mode to shore up potentially bad relations with the R.N.s.

Thus, in 1967, a two-year physician assistant program was developed within the Department of Community Health Sciences at Duke Medical Center based upon the apprentice method of teaching. Dr. Stead did not even promote the concept that an undergraduate college degree was a necessary prerequisite; it was more important that you were a devoted soldier who was prepared to work hard for many years. The PA student would not be likely to generate large debts like the medical student, because the training would only last for two years. The program would leave out a part of the medical student's general education, especially the problem-solving portion of education; that ultimate strategizing part would still remain part of the learning physician's terrain.

To fully understand the PA concept of education, one must be able to distinguish between learning the 'medicine of today' which is the known knowledge in the care of people, and the 'medicine of tomorrow'-what is not known and is concerned with problem-solving. The application of the 'medicine of today' requires teaching skills to an assistant by the apprentice method and frees up time for thinking and definitive problem-solving for the doctor.

Still, Stead wanted to keep options open to the PA student. He imagined, in that *Annals* article printed over 20 years ago, that PA-Cs might elect to obtain more years of training and evolve into physicians. Flexibility was also built into this educational endeavor in that the multiple members of the health care team spread out patient management; each worker providing a shock-absorbing function for other team members besides offering the patient a unique clinical skill. Further flexibility was promoted at the undergraduate level by proposing to admit a broader array of college students to the medical university. As Stead explained: "...[in] a true university laboratory...[students] will learn the culture of sick and well persons...the culture of medicine...[and] we will produce doctors with a wide diversity of interests and skills."

Trying to Work with Nursing Staff

Before Drs. Stead and McIntosh started searching for possible physician assistants, Dr. Stead had dealt with the nursing staff for years, attempting to get them to grow into a more integral role in serving patients. He had relied on nurses' inputs in his final yearly assessment of residents and those young doctors that could not get along with the nursing staff would tend to disappear from the Duke training system. Stead put together a breakfast meeting for nurses, analogous to morning report, with him, all the ward residents and chief resident; a meeting in which the nurses could express their dilemmas and feelings. He tried to start a program in which he apprenticed nurses to adopt greater diagnostic skills to apply 'the medicine of today.' These and other efforts were done to try to incorporate nurses more completely as 'partners' in healthcare.

So, Stead was sympathetic to the plight of nurses, but he felt that they should help generate some creative ways out of their quandary. The greatest barriers to change came from the Director of Nursing and the hospital administration at the medical center; the latter could not fathom paying nurses more for more complex skills or for more time. They both could not conceive of nurses in an expanded role and would not implement the changes in the present system that Stead desired.

Some of this inflexibility, Dr. Stead noted, was built into the nursing educational system. Nursing students had been

129

selected by admissions committees, in part, for their willingness to take orders without question; a passive characteristic. In addition, a nursing student was severely penalized for making an error; a medication error might prompt a dismissal without much chance of parole. When nursing supervisors make penalties so very severe, Stead notes, the students become overly cautious and unwilling to take initiative. Their creativity was stifled; not Dr. Stead's.

From Pathos and Photos to Movies and Slo-Mo with Time Lapse

Medical management and technology has had a progression that parallels clinical assessments and that became one basis for innovative 'Steadian' ideas. In the late '30s to the early '50s, still life, snapshot assessments in clinical practice were the agreed upon styles; reliance on pathology and anatomy made sense and was the rule. As medicine grew more sophisticated, physiology, and biochemistry joined the fray and the more realistic, moving picture art of medicine became prevalent. Cinematography became so good, you could slow down the frames, play it in different speeds, add color and contrast; you could see things that had not been seen before and you could diagnose undetected pathology. No where was this more evident than in the cardiac labs [see section on 'Gators ... ' in chapter 2]. One could say that Dr. Stead helped catalyze this entire process by involving basic sciences in medical pursuits and applying non-medical methods to patient care.

But, Dr. Stead had another idea about how to use information on a big screen, but it was not only visual data. It was data collected over many years on physicians' practices; data characterizing caring for patients with long-term problems, not just adynamic, diagnostic labels. Viewed in this manner, like time lapse photography, one could picture the development of clinical practices and commensurate healthcare needs in the community.

In Pittsburgh, his old colleague, Dr. Jack Myers was using the computer to help automate the acute care of patients; the diagnoses of hospital practice. Stead was convinced this was applying the computer to tasks that housestaff could do quite well already, albeit slower and with some hard work, which he encouraged anyway.

Rather than do this, Dr. Stead wanted to use the computer for long-term tracking of patients and for sub-grouping of them by characteristics that might affect the whole clinical course; most of it outside the hospital. That was a task that even the most gifted practitioners could not do, even those with a prodigious memory. He wanted to know how our treatments affected the long-term outcomes in people. What were the patient variables that predicted the likely outcomes?, what were the socioeconomic and cultural factors that should be considered?, could sub-classifications of clinical presentations customize our treatments effectively [remember the opening snap back in Boston?-chapter 1]?? Stead wanted markers, characteristic variations, standard deviations, outcomes research; to borrow a line from a song-'these are a few of my [the epidemiologist's] favorite things'.

There are many medical epidemiologists just down the road from Durham, residing at a rival institution in Chapel Hill; UNC. This university pioneered computer technology and housed one of the first computers worldwide in a large ventilated space. IBM aided DUMC to develop the Duke Data Bank that contains massive coronary catheter data, among other things. Now the two medical centers have large data banks that vie with each other like their basketball teams.

The Later Years

We ought to be grateful to have the benefit of being able to distill the wisdom of someone as experienced in healthcare as Dr. Eugene Stead. Although he retired from his chairmanship at Duke years ago, he has been involved with the field in other respects. He has been a consultant to The Commonwealth Fund in New York, a visiting professor of medicine at Cornell Medical School, a director of a nursing facility, a distinguished professor at the V.A. Medical Center in Durham, among other things. He has a continuing interest in the wide spectrum of activities covered by medicine; geriatrics and pediatrics. In these arenas, in particular, as well as in general internal medicine, he has become more convinced that taking care of social problems is a key part of the practice of medicine. He has always been a proponent of this, even in his earlier years when Doris Duke funded this vital effort.

He has also become more of a proponent for healthcare that affects the multitudes in this country. For some time, with the constant march of technological wonders, Dr. Stead has been in favor of preventive health measures for many [for example, nutritional programs for the needy-see chapter 11] vs. important advances that affect a limited number of individuals [such as transplants]; though, obviously, he supported both.

Dr. Stead has a deep understanding and appreciation of youth and young peoples' potential to improve the lifestyles of many. Reading of his many life experiences, one cannot help but be impressed with the fact that youthful energy can aid a person in accomplishing Herculean tasks. He strongly believes that repetition of tasks can alter the structure of neurons in the nervous system. Perhaps, the older neurons branch more with the passage of time and with continued use; and this is what we refer to as wisdom. Dr. Stead has gained more than a modicum of that commodity over the years, that's for sure.

Translation of Latin phrases: The doctor treats, nature cures.
[prior to poem]-Scholarship without morals is useless.

Considering Challenges with Dr. Stead

7

Bishops and castles and knights, oh my!; **Quotes and a Dated, Annotated C.V.**

by Robert L. Bloomfield

Don't think of retiring from the world until the world will be sorry you retire. [22] Samuel Johnson

repetitio est mater studiorum

What a person has said embodies a portion of their philosophy in an abbreviated form; like poetry. While they say 'a picture's worth a thousand words' [(1)word=(.001)picture], a quote may be worth a little less than that. Still, they lessen the number of pages that a book needs to capture an essence of something or somebody.

Many quotes attributed to Stead are noted in other books listed in the bibliography at the end of this volume. Drs. Fred Schoonmaker and Earl Metz collected some of his better-known phrases in <u>Just Say For Me,</u> which captures the more southern aspects of his eclectic influences. Dr. Stead refers to that collection as the western counterpart to Chairman Mao Tse Tung's Quotes; he calls it Chairman Stead's Red Book. Hold the Mao! Following are a few statements from Dr. Stead that I like.

135

They are taken from multiple sources, but many appear in the volume by Dr. G. Wagner, Ms. B. Cebe, and Dr. M. Rozear, What This Patient Needs is a Doctor:

Quotes:

No greater opportunity, responsibility, or obligation can fall to the lot of a human being than to become a physician. In the care of the suffering, he [or she] needs technical skill, scientific knowledge and human understanding. He [she] who uses these with courage, with humility and with wisdom will provide a unique service for his fellow man and will build an enduring edifice of character within himself [herself]. The physician should ask of his [her] destiny no more than this; he [she] should be content with no less. [26]

We have always known that the present research support mechanisms of the National Institutes of Health are not intended to solve the educational problems in the health field. In spite of this limitation, medical educators have given full support to the development of research support. The time has now come for the leaders in the research field to give as generously of their time and effort to help obtain the needed funds and facilities to provide the basic education for health personnel who can staff the areas of health service, education and research. Unless these capable leaders of research appreciate the present situation and put their best efforts into increasing the basic educational program in the medical school, they will sharply curtail the future development of their research goal. [26]

The American people and it's government are becoming progressively involved with the proper use of the "health dollar". The health dollar must provide for 1) education for health professionals, 2) delivery of health care, and 3) research at both the basic and applied levels. Public policy in the health field can be made by an informed electorate. Each person has some interest in health, the issues can be described in non-technical terms, and there are no security reasons for holding back information. [26]

I don't feel sorry for the doctor; the sick never inconvenience the well. [7]

[In a] flexible social system we have not tied income to the academic ladder; there is no papa to turn to, initiative can be taken at many levels, We don't give much, but we don't have many rules. [26]

Knowing full well the number of unsolved problems in the health field, it is obviously better judgement to restore balance to our program by increasing support in the educational and health service fields than by decreasing the rate of growth of the research program. [26]

Take care of people, not illnesses. [7]

The chief resident is the chief doctor among so many experts. Like Churchill, he's [or she's] not the brightest in any field but knows where and how to seek help when necessary. [26]

I've always thought that the best teacher placed the least limitation on his students. He [she] set the pattern for fun and satisfaction and inspired continued learning after he [she] had disappeared. Finally, he [she] must make himself [herself] dispensable so that the student can grow up and become independent of him [or her]. [26]

The secret to running a successful medical department depends on the chief assembling about him [her] a number of people, any of whom can outdistance him [her] in some field. This also must be done without arousing anxiety and jealousy, if it is to be accomplished. [26]

One learns by asking oneself questions; then going out and finding the answers. [7]

Tact, sympathy and understanding are expected of the physician, for the patient is no mere collection of symptoms, signs, disordered functions, seeking relief, help and reassurance. To the physician, as to the anthropologist, nothing human is strange or

137

repulsive. He [she] cares for people because he cares for them. [26]

Sure, we can dramatically save your life, but then you'll go on and undramatically die of something else. [26]

If you can't get your work done in 24 hours, you'd better work nights. [26]

> The weller you are, the more drugs you can take without getting sick. That's why doctors don't get into more trouble than they do with therapy. [7]

If you're going to enjoy the health professions, you have to develop a true tolerance for your fellow man [person]. [26]

A doctor is at the beck and call. If he [she] worries about himself [or herself], he [she] is not going to be a good physician. Staying up all night is only one of the hazards. [26]

One interesting thing about all patients' behavior is that they want to behave like a good patient and good family should behave. We have to make clear to them how a good family should behave. [26]

> Learning is an active process and each of us learns more when we teach than when we are taught. [7]

A doctor doesn't really need much knowledge, as he [she] can look up most things. But he must have much emotional stability and ability to perform in an air of uncertainty. [26]

Doctors forget what they know over time, even though they become wiser. On Boards, the senior student is apt to do best. [26]

> I would rather be called to see someone who is frightened than to see someone who is dying. The results of treating the first are obviously so much better. [7]

I've always felt that it is important in a curriculum to have available for a medical student a flexible period where he [or she] may spend time working with someone on the senior staff in depth, in order to learn quickly if he [she] has any aptitude or interest in laboratory medicine. [26]

The art of medicine is not confined to organic disease; it deals with the mind of the patient and with his behavior; a thinking, feeling human being. The essential skills depend not simply on instruction but on emotional maturity manifest by sensitive self-cultivation of the ability to see deeply and accurately the problems of another human being. The challenge is further magnified by the fact that the examining physician is a human instrument, subject to error due to the events in his [or her] own biography. [26]

> Only happy workers are effective recruiters of our next generation of doctors. [7]

The main thing to get out of medical school is a feeling of satisfaction with medicine. If so, the patterns developed will continue through life. It matters not the numbers of facts you accumulate in school. [26]

One cannot be nervous about the student's ignorance. If he [or she] is learning one thing well, he [she] is certainly not learning in many other areas. Our hope is that he [she] will gain freedom and that he [she] will learn to solve problems. The value of this program has to be evaluated in terms of fun and satisfaction. If the reward is considerable, the process will be repeated many times. If it is done only because the faculty requires it, the student might as well sleep through medical school. If he [or she] is going to sleep the rest of his life, no harm is done by taking a slight head start in medical school. [26]

> A doctor ought to be able to tell when a dying patient has stopped suffering so that he can direct his [or her] attention to the suffering family. [7]

I have never tried to convert medical students into textbooks. If we did, we would clearly be forced to lower tuition since the best composite of medical knowledge can be purchased for about $150. [26]

There are many ways to teach and many ways to learn. I've always felt that it is important for a student to be on a ward early in his [or her] education so that he [she] can see what doctors do and get a chance to manipulate his [her] own ideas. Perhaps it would then be possible to later revisit the basic science area at a time when it would be more relevant. [26]

The public needs to know about the basic difference between the effective program for delivering health care (the medicine of today) and the development of programs which remove the problem (research and the medicine of tomorrow). The differences in these two approaches can be told in very graphic terms. We can try, and are trying, to devise better systems to care for the people now suffering from congenital defects produced by rubella. This can be contrasted with the elimination of this problem by vaccination. [26]

Medicaid is a striking example of the passage of law without adequate information being available to the Congress or Executive branch. In the absence of a uniform federal-state system of data gathering, there was no possible way to estimate the actual impact and cost of this legislation on health care. This legislation was proposed and passed by the Congress. They had to pass it or not pass it. No mechanism existed to field test in advance any of the component parts. There are already a great many laws affecting the health field, and each year there will be more. Doctors out in the field are aware of the problems created by these laws and by the operating agencies produced by them. Once the laws are put into operation, they gain support at the agency level. The new agencies, and the personnel employed by them, become part of the large governmental bureaucracy. Regardless of the absurdities which develop, or the lack of progress in achieving the goals which the lawmakers envisaged, the new agencies will not disappear.[26]

It's hard separating functional and organic because both produce anatomical changes. We are what we are because of structure. [7]

The dying in cardiovascular disease is determined by the heart. What one does when he [or she] has cardiovascular disease is determined by the brain. [26]

You have to know the culture of the system as well as the science of the system in order for things to work at all. [26]

By reading the obituary pages...we discover that professors of preventative medicine and leaders of the American Heart Association die at the same age as their unscientific business associates. [26]

The man [person] who must know every fact, who is destroyed if he [she] must admit ignorance, is at the mercy of everyone who asks him [her] a question. [26]

Biological systems are not changed by the academic rank, harsh words or the most recent article read. [26]

I have always thought the last part of education is always more fun than the first, and you like it better when you're older. [26]

If you're doing what you want to do, you're never tired.[7]

I'm not so immune to the simple pleasures of life that I don't enjoy hearing a young man [or woman] say that he [she] has learned a lot from me but, realistically, I know it's not so. Bright men [and women] teach themselves. [26]

A good clinician ceases to make a distinction between work and play. A child equates play with good and work with bad. When a physician does this, clinical medicine becomes intolerable for him [or her]. [26]

Curriculum Vitae
[in part, from reference 26]

Birthplace and date: Decatur, GA next to Atlanta; October 6, 1908

Education: B.S., 1928, Emory University
M.D., 1932, Emory University
Experience: 1932-33: Intern, Medicine, Peter Bent Brigham Hospital
1933-34 Research Fellow, Medicine Harvard
1934-35: Intern, Surgery, Peter Bent Brigham Hospital
1935-36: Assistant Resident, Medicine, Cincinnati General Hospital
1936-37: Resident, Medicine, Cincinnati General Hospital
1937-39: Assistant in Medicine, Harvard and Boston City Hospital
1939-41: Instructor in Medicine, Peter Bent Brigham Hospital
1941-42: Associate in Medicine, Harvard
1942-46: Professor of Medicine and Chairman, Department of Medicine, Emory University
1945-46: Dean, Emory University School of Medicine
1947-67: Professor of Medicine and Chairman, Department of Medicine, Duke University
1967-1999: Professor of Medicine, Duke University

Other Activities:
Past Secretary and past President, Association of American Physicians
Past Secretary and past President, American Society for Clinical Investigation
Master, American College of Physicians
Member, Association of University Cardiologists
Member, American Heart Association
Past Member, Research Allocations Committee, American Heart Association
Past Chairman, Ethics Committee, American Heart Association
Founding Member, National Academy of Sciences Institute of Medicine
Past Member, Panel on Space Science and Technology [NASA] of the President's Science Advisory Committee
Member, American Medical Association
Past Member, Council of the National Heart Institute
Past Member, Council of the National Institute of Arthritis and Metabolic Diseases

Past Consultant to National Heart Institute, Artificial Heart and Myocardial Infarction Program

Past Member, Advisory Council, Life Insurance Medical Research Fund

Past Director, Regenstrief Foundation for Research in Health Care

Editor, *CIRCULATION*, American Heart Association, 1973-78

Established training program for physician's assistants at Duke University

Phi Beta Kappa

Alpha Omega Alpha

Distinguished Professor, Duke University

Honorary Fellow, American College of Cardiology

Citation for Distinguished Service to Research, American Heart Association, 1959

The John M. Russell Award, Markle Foundation, 1968

Distinguished Teacher Award, American College of Physicians, 1969

The Robert H. Williams Award, Association of Professors of Medicine, 1970

James B. Herrick Award, American Heart Association, 1970

Abraham Flexner Award for Distinguished Service to Medical Education, Association of American Medical Colleges, 1970

Founder's Award, Southern Society for Clinical Investigation, 1973

Honorary degree: Doctor of Science, Emory University, 1968

Honorary degree: Doctor of Science, Yale University, 1971

Distinguished Teaching Award, Duke Medical Alumni Association, 1974

Georgia Heart Association, Symposium in Honor of Eugene Stead, 1976

Gold Heart Award, American Heart Association, 1976

More Activities and Accessory Interests:

Editorial Advisory Board, Classics of Medicine Library, 1941-present

Distinguished Professor of Medicine, Duke VA, 1978-85

Visiting Professor of Medicine, Cornell Medical School, New York City, 1968

Commonwealth Fund, NYC, 1968
Aided reorganization of Baylor Medical School with Dr. DeBakey, Houston, TX, 1968
Editor, *North Carolina Medical Journal*, 1983-92

Extramural activities:
building, pottery, antique lamps, directing careers in health sciences, writing textbooks, reading, reading, reading.

Publications [abridged list]:

... you will find once in five centuries of waiting, one majestic head which overtops the highest.... ... you have the here and there man that is larger-brained...; you have the still rarer man of ... wider and more lasting distinction; and in that final head rising solitary out of the stretch of ages, you have the limit of Nature's output.

from Mark Twain in *Letters from the Earth   [26]*

Dr. S. indicates Dr. Stead

Bryan, Evans, Fulton, and Dr. S. Diuresis following the administration of salyrgan. Arch. Int. Med. 55: 735-744, 1935

Gregerson, Gibson, and Dr. S. Plasma volume determination with dyes: errors in colorimetry; use of the blue dye T-1824. Am. J. Physiol. 113: No.1, September 1935.

Dr. S. and Kunkel. A plethysmographic method for the quantitative measurement of blood flow in the foot. J. Clin. Invest. 17: 711, 1983.

Kunkel and Dr. S. Blood Flow and vasomotor reactions in the foot in health, in arteriosclerosis, and in thromboangitis obliterans. J. Clin. Invest. 17: 715, 1938.

Kunkel, Dr. S., and Weiss. Blood flow and vasomotor reactions in the hand, forearm, foot and calf in response to physical and chemical stimuli. J. Clin. Invest. 18: 225, 1939.

Dr. S. and Kunkel Influence of the peripheral circulation in the upper extremity on the circulation time as measured by the sodium cyanide method. Am. J. Med. Sci. 198: 49, 1939.

Dr. S. and Kunkel. Mechanism of the arterial hypertension induced by paredrinol. J. Clin. Invest. 18: 439, 1939.

Dr. S. and Kunkel. Factors influencing the auricular murmur and the intensity of the first heart sound. Am. Heart J. 18: 261, 1939.

Dr. S., Kunkel, and Weiss. Effect of pitressin in circulatory collapse induced by sodium nitrate. J. Clin. Invest. 18: 673, 1939.

Dr. S. and Weiss. Effect of paredrinol on sodium nitrate collapse and on clinical shock. J. Clin. Invest. 18: 679, 1939. [see ch.2]

When Dr. Stead first arrived in Durham, he was assigned a secretary named Sally ['Skip'] Verner. She was married to a first year medical student named John Verner. She left her position after six months due to pregnancy, but her husband graduated from Duke Medical School. Dr. Stead recalls that John was one of his favorite students and that he went travelling, after graduation, on Stead's suggestion, to complete his first year of residency at the University of Michigan. Stead advised him to do this to prove to this admirable young doctor that Duke was the best place for him and many others. After completing this year, John begged Stead to accept him back to Durham, which the chairman gladly did. John spent about the next twenty years at Duke Medical Center as a stellar clinician on the faculty.

Dr. S. and Kunkel. Nature of peripheral resistance in arterial hypertension. J. Clin. Invest. 19:25, 1940.

Dr. S. and Kunkel. Absorption of sulphanilamide as an index of the blood flow in the intestine of man. Am. J. Med. Sci. 199: 680, 1940.

Ebert and Dr. S. The effect of the application of tourniquets on the hemodynamics of circulation. J. Clin. Invest. 19: 561, 1940.

Dr. S. and Ebert. in: The peripheral circulation in acute infectious diseases. Med. Clin. North America 24: 1387, 1940.

Dr. S. Changes in circulation produced by poor postural adaptation. Bull. New England Med. Center 2: 290, 1940.

Ramano, Dr. S., and Taylor Clinical and Electroencephalographic changes produced by a sensitive carotid sinus of the cerebral type. New England J. Med. 223: 708, 1940.

Ebert , and Dr. S. An error in measuring changes in plasma volume after exercise. Proc. Soc. Exper. Biol. & Med. 46: 139, 1941.

Dr. John Verner was just one of many who made their mark in Durham. Verner was loved by many, though some in the Department of Psychiatry questioned his qualifications to deal with some 'psychiatric' patient problems. According to Stead, John was very good with people; even before he obtained his medical degree. Patients enjoyed his brand of 'psychiatric' attention, talking with them, analyzing their problems, and suggesting treatments; even when he was a mere medical student. Disagreements among some Psychiatry Department faculty members and the Medicine Department, concerning these issues, led to his subsequent move to Florida. His leaving remains one of Stead's rare regrets to this day.

Dr. S. and Ebert. The action of paredrinol after induction of hemorrhage and circulatory collapse. Am. J. Med. Sci. 201: 396, 1941.

Dr. S., and Ebert. Postural hypotension; a disease of the sympathetic nervous system. Arch. Int. Med. 67: 546, 1941.

Ebert and Dr. S. Demonstration that in normal man no reserves of blood are mobilized by exercise, epinephrine and hemorrhage. Am. J. Med. Sci. 201: 655, 1941.

Ebert and Dr. S. Demonstration that the cell plasma ratio of blood contained in minute vessels is lower than that of venous blood. J. Clin. Invest. 20: 317, 1941.

Dr. S. The treatment of circulatory collapse and shock. Am. J. Med. Sci. 210: 775, 1941.

Ebert and Dr. S. Circulatory failure in acute infections. J. Clin. Invest. 20: 671, 1941.

Ebert, Dr. S., and Gibson. Response of normal subjects to acute blood loss. Arch. Int. Med. 68: 578, 1941.

Schales, Ebert, and Dr. S. Capillary tube Kjeldahl method for determining protein content of 5 to 20 milligrams of Tussie fluid. Proc. Soc. Exper. Biol. & Med. 49: 1, 1942.

Dr. S. and Ebert. Shock syndrome produced by failure of the heart. Arch. Int. Med. 69: 369, 1942. [see ch. 2]

Ebert, Dr. S., Warren, and Watts. Plasma protein replacement after hemorrhage in dogs with and without shock. Am. J. Physiol. 136: 299, 1942.

Dr. Verner worked well with students and colleagues. He collaborated with others very well, too. He is credited with describing a clinical, endocrinologic syndrome with a Duke pathologist, Dr. Morrison. Verner-Morrison Syndrome, as it is still referred to, is a symptom complex associated with a tumor involving the pancreas. The study of symptomatology and understanding the subtle differences in clinical presentation that this demonstrates is a credit to the person who described it and to the philosophy that encouraged such scholarship.

Dr. S, Ebert, Ramano, and Warren. Central autonomic paralysis. Arch. Neurol. Psychiat. 48: 92, 1942.

Warren, Walter, Ramano, and Dr. S. Blood flow in the hand and forearm after paravertebral block of the sympathetic ganglia. Evidence against sympathetic vasodilator nerves in the extremities of man. J. Clin. Invest. 21: 665, 1942.

Schales, Dr. S., and Warren. Nonspecific effect of certain kidney extracts in lowering blood pressure. Am. J. Med. Sci. 204: 797, 1942.

Warren and Dr. S. The effect of the accumulation of blood in the extremities on the venous pressure of normal subjects. Am. J. Med. Sci. 205: 501, 1943.

Weiss, Dr. S., Warren, and Bailey. Scleroderma heart disease. Arch. Int. Med. 71: 749, 1943.

Dr. S. and Warren. Clinical significance of hyperventilation: the role of hyperventilation in the production, diagnosis and treatment of certain anxiety symptoms. Am. J. Med. Sci. 206: 183, 1943.

Warren, Merrill, and Dr. S. The role of extracellular fluid in the maintenance of a normal plasma volume. J. Clin. Invest. 22: 635, 1943.

Dr. S. The pathologic physiology of generalized circulatory failure and of cardiac pain. In: A Textbook of Medicine. Ed: Cecil, 6th ed., W.B. Saunders Co., Phila., 1943, pp. 1017-1030.

Dr. S. Circulatory Collapse and Shock. In: A Textbook of Medicine. Ed: Cecil, 6th ed., W.B. Saunders C. Phila., 1943, pp. 1199-1202.

Warren and Dr. S. Fluid dynamics in chronic congestive heart failure. Arch. Int. Med. 73: 138, 1944.

Dr. S. and Warren. The effect of the injection of histamine into the brachial artery on the permeability of the capillaries of the forearm and hand. J. Clin. Invest. 23: 279, 1944.

Dr. S. and Warren. The protein content of the extracellular fluid in normal subjects after venous congestion and in patients with cardiac failure, anoxemia and fever. J. Clin. Invest. 23: 283, 1944.

As far as we know, Dr. Verner and his wife, Sally, led very full, comfortable existences in the "City of Medicine". When they lived in North Carolina, they always resided in very nice surroundings and abodes; more sumptuous than many medical faculty members. When they moved to Florida, John became director of Sally's family's business- distributing fruit. While we don't fully understand this transition, Dr. Verner has told Dr. Stead that years in medicine helped him immensely in his business pursuits. Actually, one of Stead's first chief residents, Dr. Sam Martin, got an additional degree at the London's School of Economics after becoming Chairman of Medicine at the University of Florida at Gainseville. Dr. Martin taught for many years after leaving medicine at The Wharton School of Finance at The University of Pennsylvania in Philadelphia. The challenges sometimes never completely stop for some scholarly teachers; not even in the medical field.

Dr. S. and Warren. Care of the patient with chronic heart disease. Med. Clin. North America 28: 381, 1944.

Warren, Dr. S., Merrill, and Brannon. Chemical, clinical and immunological studies of the products of human plasma fractionation. IX. The treatment of shock with concentrated human serum albumin: a preliminary report. J. Clin. Invest. 23: 506, 1944.

Warren and Dr. S. The protein content of edema fluid in patients with acute glomerulonephritis. Am. J. Med. Sci. 208: 618, 1944.

Cooper, Dr. S., and Warren. the beneficial effect of intravenous infusions in acute pericardial tamponade. Ann. Surg. 120: 822, 1944.

Dr. S. and Warren. Orientation to the mechanisms of clinical shock. Arch. Surg. 50:1, 1945.   [see ch. 2]

Dr. S., Warren, Merrill, and Brannon. The cardiac output in male subjects as measured by the technique of right atrial catheterization. J. Clin. Invest. 44: 326, 1945.

"There are two kinds of students that the gods give me. One kind they dump on me like a bushel of potatoes. I do not like potatoes, and the potatoes they do not ever seem to have great affection for me, but I take them and teach them to kill patients. The other kind--they are very few!--they seem for some reason that is not at all clear to me to wish a liddle bit to become scientists, to work with bugs and make mistakes. Those, ah, those, I seize them, I denounce them, I teach them right away the ultimate lesson of science, which is to wait and doubt. Of the potatoes, I demand nothing; of the foolish ones like you, who think I could teach them something, I demand everything. No. You are too young. Come back next year."

from Arrowsmith by Sinclair Lewis, 1925, 1st ed., P. F. Collier Pub., New York, pp. 12

Brannon, Merrill, Warren, and Dr. S. The cardiac output of patients with chronic anemia as measured by the technique of right atrial catheterization. J. Clin. Invest. 44: 332, 1945.

Warren, Brannon, Dr. S., and Merrill. The effect of venesection and the pooling of blood in the extremities on the atrial pressure and cardiac outputin normal subjects with observations on acute circulatory collapse in three instances. J. Clin. Invest. 44: 337, 1945.

These students have met in classes and done exercises not related to any service function all of their lives. They need to be listened to, not talked to. They need to use words, handle ideas, discover the ways of building different houses from the same blocks, discover the noise in the communications system, and identify the differences between memory and thinking.

E. A. Stead

Dr. S. Shock syndrome in internal medicine. in: Oxford Medicine 2: 13, 1945.

Warren, Dr. S., and Brannon. The cardiac output in man: a study of some of the errors in the method of right heart catheterization. Am. J. Physiol. 145: 458, 1946.

Brannon, Dr. S., Warren, and Merrill. Hemodynamics of acute hemorrage in man. Am. Heart J. 31: 407, 1946.

Merrill, Warren, Dr. S., and Brannon. The circulation in penetrating wounds of the chest: a study by the methods of right heart catheterization. Am. Heart J. 31: 413, 1946.

Warren, Brannon, Dr. S., and Merrill. Pericardial tamponade from stab wound of the heart and pericardial effusion of empyema: a study utilizing the method of right catheterization. Am. Heart J. 31: 418, 1946.

Dr. S., Brannon, Merrill, and Warren. Concentrated human albumin in the treatment of shock. Arch. Int. Med. 77: 564, 1946.

Dr. S., Hickam, and Warren. Mechanism for changing the cardiac output in man. Trans. Asso. Am. Phys. 60: 74, 1947.

Dr. S. and Warren. Cardiac output in man. An analysis of the mechanisms varying the cardiac outpatient based on recent clinical studies. Arch. Int. Med. 80: 237, 1947.   [see ch. 2]

Dr. S. Fainting. In: Signs and Symptoms. Ed: MacBryde. Lippincott, Phila., 1947, pp. 179-187.

Dr. S. Relation of the cardiac output to the symptoms and signs of congestive heart failure. Modern Concepts of Cardiovasc. Dis. 16: No. 12, 1947.

Warren, Brannon, Weens, and Dr. S. Effect of increasing the blood volume and right atrial pressure on the circulation of normal subjects by intravenous infusions. Am. J. Med. 4: 192, 1948.

Change is always more troublesome than sitting still. Change is most easily accomplished at the medical school-college interface or in the first two years of medical school. Innovation at this level will never have much effect on the educational program, because the majority of a doctor's education comes after that period of time. Any significant change will have to affect the clinical years of medical school, internship, residency and postgraduate education.

E. A. Stead

153

Scheinberg, Robertson, and Dr. S. The relation between atrial pressure and blood flow in the foot. Am. Heart. J. 35: 409, 1948.

Dr. S.,Warren, and Brannon. Cardiac output in congestive heart failure. Am. Heart J. 35: 529, 1948.

Dr. S., Warren, and Brannon. Effect of lanatoside C on the circulation of patients with congestive heart failure. Arch. Int. Med. 81: 282, 1948.

Scheinberg and Dr. S. The cerebral blood flow in subjects as measured by the nitrous oxide technique. Normal values for blood flow, oxygen utilization, glucose utilization, and peripheral resistance, with observations on the effect of tilting and anxiety . J. Clin. Invest. 28: 1163, 1949.

Dr.S. Edema of heart failure. Bull. New York Acad. Med. 24: 607, 1948.

Dr. S. The role of cardiac output in the mechanisms of congestive heart failure. Am. J. Med. 6: 232, 1949.   [see ch. 2]

Scheinberg, Dr. S., Brannon, and Warren. Correlative observations on cerebral metabolism and cardiac output in myxedema. J. Clin. Invest. 29: 1139, 1950.

Dr. S., Meyers, Scheinberg, Cargill, Hickam, and Levitan. Studies of cardiac output and of blood flow and metabolism of splanchnic area, brain and kidney. Trans. Asso. Am. Phys. 63: 241, 1950.

Dr. S. Circulatory Collapse and shock. In: <u>Textbook of Medicine</u>. Ed: Cecil & Loeb. W.B. Saunders Co., Phila., 1951, pp. 1211-1214.

Many facts are best left in books.

Medicine is a service profession. The doctor agrees that patients can make demands on him [or her]-both reasonable and unreasonable-and that he [she] will meet these needs. The student must determine whether he [she] is comfortable with sick people, whether he [she] can meet their multiple needs and still enjoy the day.

E. A. Stead

Dr. S. Pathologic, Physiology of Generalized Circulatory Failure. The Treatment of Congestive Heart Failure, Cardiac Dilatation and Hypertrophy. In: <u>Textbook of Medicine</u>. Ed: Cecil & Loeb. W.B. Saunders Co., Phila., 1951, pp. 1051-1066.

Dr. S. Renal factors in congestive heart failure. Circulation 3: 294, 1951.

Dr. S. Cerebral blood flow and metabolism. Am. J. Med. 9: 425, 1950.

Murphy and Dr. S. Effects of exogenous and endogenous posterior pituitary antidiuretic hormone on water and electrolyte excretion. J. Clin. Invest. 30: 1055, 1951.

Dr. S. Edema and dyspnea of heart failure. Bull. New York Acad. Med. 28: 159, 1952.

Holland and Dr. S. Effect of vasopression (pitressin)-induced water retention on sodium excretion. Arch. Int. Med. 88: 571, 1951.

Bell and Dr. S. Effects of epinephrine on the vessels of the calf. Observations on the period of initial vasodilation. J. Appl. Physiol. 5: 228, 1952.

Dr. S. Fainting. Am. J. Med. 13: 387, 1952.

Dr. S. Presidential Address: Proc. 45th Annual Meeting, American Society for Clinical Investigation, May 1953. J. Clin. Invest. 32: 548, 1953.

Dr. S. Peripheral Vascular Disease. In: <u>Textbook of Medicine</u>. Ed: Cecil & Loeb. Blakinston, New York, 1954, pp. 1437-1448.

Dr. S. General Consideration of Pain. In: <u>Principles of Internal Medicine</u>. Ed: Harrison. McGraw-Hill, New York, 1954, pp. 17-20.

In the practice of medicine the physician employs a discipline which seeks to use scientific methods and principles in the solution of it's problems, but it is one which in the end remains an art. It is an art in the sense that rarely, if ever, can the individual patient be considered the equivalent of an experiment so completely controlled that it is possible to exclude judgement and experience from the interpretation of the patients reaction.

E. A. Stead

Holland and Dr. S. Electrolyte excretion after single doses of ACTH, cortisone, desoxycorticosterone glucoside and motionless standing. J. Clin. Invest. 33: 132, 1954.

Dr. S. Ciculatory Collapse and Shock. In: <u>Textbook of Medicine</u>. Ed: Cecil & Loeb. W. B. Saunders Co. Phila., 9th ed., 1955, pp. 1261-1264.

Dr. S. Diseases of the Circulatory System. In: <u>Textbook of Medicine</u>. Ed: Cecil & Loeb. W. B. Suanders Co. Phila., 9th ed., 1955, pp. 1230-1246.

In a way interns are like patients with rheumatoid arthritis. Both have their limitation, and one has to learn to live with them.

It is very hard to go home and think great thoughts when you are bone tired from being in the clinic or operating room all day.
E. A. Stead

Dr. S. and Hickam. in: <u>Heart Failure. Disease-a-Month</u>. Year Book Publishers, Inc., Chicago, 1955, pp. 3-32.

Burnum, Hickam, and Dr. S. Hyperventilation in postural hypotention. Circulation 10: 362, 1954.

Dr. S. Fainting (Syncope). In: <u>Signs and Symptoms</u>. Ed: MacBryde. Lippincott, 3rd ed., 1957, pp. 665-678.

Dr. S. and Wallace. Reactivity of small blood vessels. Trans. Asso. .Am. Phys. 70: 275, 1957.

Orgain and Dr. S. Congestive heart failure. Circulation 16: 291, 1957.

Wallace and Dr. S. Spontaeous pressure evaluations in small veins and effects of norepinephrine and cold. Circul. Res. 5: 650, 1957.

Dr. S. Peripheral Vascular Disease. In: <u>Principles of Internal Medicine</u>, McGraw-Hill, New York, 1958, pp. 1339-1348.

Dr. S. Disease of the Cardiovascular System. Circulatory Collapse and Shock. In: <u>Textbook of Medicine</u>, Ed: Cecil & Loeb, 10th ed., W.B. Saunders, Phila., 1959, pp. 1172-1187 and 1199-1202.

Wallace and Dr. S. Fall in pressure in radial artery during reactive hyperemia. Circul. Res. 7: 876, 1959.

Dr. S. Hyperventilation. Disease-a-Month, February 1960, pp. 5-31.

Wallace, Garcia, and Dr. S. Arteriovenous differences of the norepinephrine-like material from plasma infused norepinephrine. J. Clin. Invest. 40: 1387, 1961.

Gorten, Gunnells, Weissler, and Dr. S. Effects of atropine and isoproterenol on cardiac output, central venous pressure and mean transit time of indicators placed at three different sites in the venous system. Circul. Res. 9: 979, 1961.

As advanced students of clinical medicine, interns and residents of necessity perform some service. What should they be paid? The idea of paying them primarily for service has never been seriously proposed for one simple reason: the intern and resident can create more funds by practice than the hospital can collect for their services. Even if 100% of the income created by the residents were collected, they would still be underpaid.

E. A. Stead

Dr. S. Pain in the extremities. In: <u>Principles of Internal Medicine.</u> Ed: Harrison. McGraw-Hill, New York, 1962, pp. 56-60.

Dr. S. Medical Care: it's social and organizational aspects. Postgraduate medical education in the hospital. New England J. Med. 269: 240, 1963.

Dr. S. The evaluation of the medical university. J. Med. Educ. 39: 368, 1964.

Dr. S. Preparation for practice. Pharos of AOA 29: 70, 1966.

Dr. S. Current Concepts. Training and use of paramedical personnel. New England J. Med. 277: 800, 1967.

Dr. S. Educational programs and manpower. Bull. New York Acad. Med. 44: 204, 1968.

Dr. S. More knowledge about renal factors influencing sodium excretion. Editorial. Medical Times 96: 665, 1968.

Dr. S. The limitations of teaching. Pharos of AOA 32: 54, 1969.

Dr. S. What we have learned about myocardial infarction from epidemiologic and dietary studies. Circulation 40: IV-85, 1969.

Dr. S. The role of the university in graduate training. J. Med. Educ. 44: 739, 1969.

Dr. S. Pain in the Extremities. In: <u>Harrison's Principles of Internal Medicine.</u> Ed: Wintrobe. McGraw-Hill, New York, pp. 79-81, 1970.

To be an effective physician one must be able to give of himself [or herself] without resentment. Patients must be free to make demands on him [or her] when they are socially least attractive.

Two years in a hospital, night and day, are necessary to see how illness looks-to see what the people behind the patient look like in all circumstances.

E. A. Stead

Dr. S. Vascular Disease of the Extremities. In: <u>Harrison's Principles of Inernal Medicine.</u> Ed: Wintrobe. McGraw-Hill, New York, pp. 1265-1274, 1970.

Dr.S. Fainting (Syncope). In: <u>Signs and Symptoms.</u> Ed: MacBryde. Lippincott, Philadelphia, pp. 712-721, 1970.

Dr. S. A proposal for the creation of a compulsory national service corps. Arch. Int. Med. 127: 89, 1971.

Dr. S. Why moon walking is simpler than social progress. Pharos AOA 34: 3, 1971.

Dr. S. Physicians--past and future. Arch. Int. Med. 127: 703, 1971.

In our medical school I always assume that our graduates will take care of sick and well people. No amount of research aptitude or interest expressed by the man [or woman] in training persuades us that he [or she] will not eventually doctor. The rewards, emotional and intellectual, of doctoring are too high.

E. A. Stead

Dr. S. Use of physicians' assistants in the delivery of medical care. Ann. Rev. Med. 22: 273, 1971.

Dr. S. Editor: with Smythe, Gunn, and Littlemeyer. Educational technology for medicine: roles for the Lister Hill Center. J. Med. Educ. 46: 11-93, 1971.

Rosati, Wallace, and Dr. S. The way of the future. Arch. Int. Med. 1 1: 285, 1973.

Anlyan, Austen, Beck, Bradford, Brown, Cherkasky, Elam, Kinney, London, Medrearis, Dr. S., and Kloot. in: The Future of Medical Education. Duke University Press, !973. 192.pp.

Dr. S. Chapter in: Hippocrates Revisited. Ed: R.J. Bulger. Medcom Press, New York, 1973. 2 8 pp.

Dr. S. Walter Kempner: a perspective. Arch. Int. Med. 133: 755, 1974.

[To Harvard Dean]: I have made the decision to accept the Commonwealth's offer to use their facilities as my base of operation for 1968. I lived in Boston in the days of my youth. I'd better leave my memories untainted by reality and the cold light of more advanced years. I am both pleased and honored that you would have been willing to arrange a year at Harvard [1967]. [26]

E. A. Stead

Translation of Latin phrase: Repetition is the mother of studies.

Considering Challenges with Dr. Stead

8

Strategy; **Excerpts From Two Addresses by Osler and an Historical Note**

by Robert L. Bloomfield

One of the signs of truly educated people, and a broadly educated nation, is lack of prejudice. [22] Charles H. Mayo.

No one affected many of the changes in the practice of medicine more than Sir William Osler. Dr. Stead carried on this tradition and broadened it as well.

Address by Osler to The Academy of Medicine, New York, 1903, adapted from the speech-**'Hospital as a College'**:

The pupil handles a sufficient number of cases to get certain measure of technical skill, and there is ever kept before him the idea that he is not in the hospital to learn everything that is known but to learn how to study disease and how to treat it, or rather, how to treat patients. A third change is in reorganization of the medical school. There are hundreds of earnest students, thousands of patients, and scores of well equipped young men willing and anxious to do practical teaching. ...for the bread of the wards they are given the stones of the lecture room and amphitheatre. The dissociation of students and patient is a legacy of the pernicious system of theoretical teaching from which we have escaped in the first and second years. For the third and fourth year students, the hospital is the college; They should be in it as the place in which alone they can learn the elements of their

art and the lessons which will be of service to them when in practice.... The hospital with students in its dispensaries and wards doubles its usefulness in a community. The stimulus of their presence neutralizes that clinical apathy certain, sooner or later, to beset the man who makes lonely "rounds" with his house physician. The practical education of young men, who carry with them to all parts of the country good methods, extends enormously the work of an institution, and the profession is recruited by men who have been taught to think and to observe for themselves. It is no new method of which I advocate, but the old method of Boerhaave, of the elder Rutherford of the Edinburgh school, of the older men of this city, and of Boston and of Philadelphia. It makes of the hospital a college in which the students slowly learn for themselves. It is the true method, because it is the natural one, the only one by which a physician grows in clinical wisdom after he begins practice for himself....
[24]

There can be no adequate technical education which is not liberal and no liberal education which is not technical.   [22]
Alfred North Whitehead

In May of 1905, Sir William Osler gave his farewell address, "L'ENVOI", to a gathering of physicians from the U.S. and Canada before his departure to Oxford in Great Britain. In that address, he stated, "But of this I am certain:-If there is one thing above another which needs a change in this country, it is the present hospital system in relation to the medical school." Five years later Abraham Flexner would publish his revealing report on medical education. The report, funded by the Carnegie Foundation found that only one out of 155 medical schools reviewed in the U.S. and Canada provided an acceptable medical

164

education at that time: Johns Hopkins Medical School, where Osler recently held a professorship.

Years after this critical report, Flexner would be named the first director of the Institute for Advanced Study in Princeton, N.J., a community of scientists and scholars. The Institute still includes programs in historical studies and social sciences in addition to the customary basic sciences. Faculty and students are given much intellectual freedom. There are no examinations and no degrees; knowledge is pursued, primarily, for the love of learning.

In 1933, the director for the program in mathematical research was appointed, Dr. Albert Einstein. As he said in his later years, "it's a good thing to show those who are striving alongside of us, how one's own striving and searching appears to one in retrospect." He was not the only calculating genius that believed in the need for a unified system for all and learning from a review of the past.

Address by Osler to McGill Medical School students, 1894, adapted from the speech-**'Teaching and Thinking'**:

The wise instruction and the splendid example of such men as Holmes,... and others have carried comfort into thousands of homes throughout this land. The benefits derived from the increased facilities in the teaching of medicine will not be confined to the citizens of this town, but will be widely diffused and felt in every locality to which the graduates of this school may go; ...every gift which promotes higher medical education, and which enables the medical faculties throughout the country to turn out better doctors, means fewer mistakes in diagnosis, greater skill in dealing with emergencies, and the saving of pain and anxiety to sufferers and their friends. The physician needs...a

165

kind heart; his work is arduous..., requiring the exercise of the very highest faculties of the mind, while constantly appealing to the emotions and finer feelings. At no time has his influence been more potent than at the present, at no time has he been so powerful a factor for good, and as it is one of the highest possible duties of a great University to fit men for this calling, so it will be your highest mission, students of medicine, to carry on the never-ending warfare against disease and death, better equipped, ... than your predecessors, but animated with their spirit and sustained by their hopes, ... The other function of the University is to think. Teaching current knowledge and teaching how to teach, form the routine work of the various college faculties. What I mean by the thinking function of the University, is that duty which the professional corps owes to enlarge the boundaries of human knowledge. Work of this sort makes a University great. In a progressive institution the changes come slowly. Everywhere the old order changeth, and happy those who can change with it. Teachers who teach current knowledge are not necessarily investigators. The very best instructor for students may have no conception of the higher lines of work in his branch, and contrariwise, how many brilliant investigators have been wretched teachers? In a school which has reached this stage and wishes to do thinking as well as teaching, men must be selected who are not only thoroughly *au courant* with the best work in their department the world over, but who also have ideas, ambition and energy to put them into force. They should be sought for far and wide; an institution which wraps itself in Strabo's cloak and does not look beyond the college gates in selecting professors may get good teachers, but rarely good thinkers. One of the chief difficulties in the way of advanced work is the stress of routine class and laboratory duties, which often sap the energies of men capable of higher things. To meet this difficulty it is essential, first, to give the professors plenty of assistance, so that they will not be worn out with teaching; and, secondly, to give encouragement to graduates and others to carry on researches under their direction. Their work is the outward ... sign that a university is thinking. Surrounded by a group of bright young minds, well trained in advanced methods, not only is the professor himself stimulated to do his best work, but he has to keep far afield and to know what is stirring in every part of his own domain. There remains now to foster that indefinable something which, for want of a better term, we call the university spirit, ...which is associated with men and not with money, which cannot be purchased in the market or grown to order, but which comes insensibly with loyal devotion to duty and to high ideals.... [24]

Osler was a great speechwriter with social insight, to say the least; Flexner wrote an institution-shattering report; Einstein wrote many mind-boggling things on a blackboard that I'll never understand, but he wrote about theoretical things that changed our views on just about everything. Around 1970, Stead wrote an article for the medical honor society, Pharos, that has a direct bearing on all these historical occurrences. The article is entitled, *Why Moon Walking is Simpler than Social Progress [20]*, but I've renamed it to be, *Why Most Writing is Simpler than Social Progress,* just for this discussion.

In May of '61, President John Kennedy stated that the U.S. would land a man on the moon by 1970. Resources were mobilized and we accomplished that goal to many people's amazement. Yet, many others vocalized frustration that, at the same time, we were not successful in our attempts to solve major problems on this planet; poverty, ignorance, war, racism, healthcare. Part of Stead's explanation was that pursuing the space program involved primarily inanimate technology and that it was possible to alter the blueprint quickly and nimbly to meet changing program needs. It didn't involve the whole population, nor did it require constant acts of congress to implement alterations. Human needs are much harder to improve than machinery or technology. To adapt a phrase from Neal Armstrong, "One step for a mensch; a giant leap for munchkins."; "Houston, we still have a problem."

Compared to effecting social change, publishing medical articles or books like this one, giving speeches, and developing medical procedures are not as difficult. Enacting legislation, running departments, building universities, and theorizing about universal laws are all very difficult, but, they're not as hard as trying to change society; no way!. To create social changes requires many resources and a strong, charismatic director as well as a community; a real superman or superwoman; an 'ubermensch' [overman], as Nietzsche calls it. 'It takes' a lot more than 'a village'; that's the truth.

tantum religio poyuit suadere malorum

Bedside Teaching

Before the establishment of Johns Hopkins Medical School in 1889 where Osler was the first chairman in the Department of Medicine, medical students were trained by lectures, not by patient experiences gained by the bedside. Osler was joined by other great faculty members; Welch in pathology, Kelly in obstetrics/ gynecology, and Halsted in surgery. Osler, and Stead after him, mistrusted lectures and surrounded themselves with great teachers in other disciplines. Osler himself had taught pathology, physiology, and histology previously. The medical

168

curriculum he organized in Baltimore was reputed to be the most rigorous in the U.S. at that time. His famous textbook of medicine was unique in that it relied on historical, anatomical, and pathologic references. According to one author [12], this book was instrumental in the early funding of medical research by the Rockefeller Foundation in 1902.

While Stead did not write any textbooks, he stimulated collaboration and research from many disciplines, sometimes from seemingly unrelated areas. While he developed a reputation as a demanding clinician in a rigorous program, he was, like Osler, also known as a compassionate diagnostician and a dedicated teacher. Those who came to enter his program were surprised to find that everyone in the department put emphasis on teaching medicine, or, at least, they were asked to. Stead believed that practitioners, even more than the academicians, would end up teaching: teaching personnel, paramedical assistants, and, above all, teaching their patients.

Teaching medicine was an effective way for Dr. Stead to promote the belief in human lives enhanced in a healthful manner so as to affirm the quality of existence. In that state, the patient would be at the peak of their vitality and creativity. Each person, patient, student, or resident, would differ in their makeup. Thus, their unique propensities and abilities would be cultivated and employed differently. What mattered most to Dr. Stead was not Medicine per se, but the enhancement of life.

Translation of Latin phrase:
         For how many evils is religion responsible.

Considering Challenges with Dr. Stead

9

Fool's mate; **Physicians of
The Past And Future**
[Your Turn]
by Robert L. Bloomfield

*A good education should
leave much to be desired.
[22] Alan Gregg*

usus te plura docebit

Medical School Education According to Stead

When it concerned medical education, Dr. Stead agreed with
Osler; the magic word was 'work'. The reputation that he
established in the medical community for the Duke medical
program was one of very hard work. Only men and women of
steel could survive a 5 out of 7 night call schedule and rumors of
grueling grilling on rounds. This 'hearsay' was free advertising
that Stead capitalized on to attract the most dedicated clinical
performers; but no residents actually died from overwork.

171

His view of the role of faculty was subordinate to stimulating these potential great performers. He was searching for basic science instructors who would actually reinforce the liberal education that the student had been exposed to in earlier college days and demonstrate that a new discipline could solve clinical problems while complementing their existent knowledge base. The basic science faculty was not there to "stuff the heads of medical students with innumerable facts...", but "...to give joy to the learning ...." The role of the basic science instruction was to impart information that the doctor needed to practice good medicine and to teach the student how to learn.

Dr. Stead wanted the impressionable student to savor the drama-tragedy and comedy-that defines human experience. Patient histories had to be obtained with precision and a repetitive method, but the good physician had to go beyond this; he or she had to be creative and not sell their souls to the latest technology. Then, they would never find practice dull. He warned them to be non-judgmental; the patients were not good and bad. They had simple and difficult problems. "[Be] kindly ... toward [those] unfortunate enough to seek medical [attention].... Leave your hostilities to the tennis court...."

The education of the doctor which goes on after ... his degree is ... the most important part of his education. J.S. Billings [22]

Practicing the Art while Keeping a Liberal Education Going

172

Advice is cheap, but even cheap advice from someone as experienced as Dr. Stead is precious indeed. So, I have distilled some sage advice for those in the medical profession from this physician/educator.

The well-educated person must be willing and able to concentrate. When 'ol' blue eyes' [as Stead has been affectionately called] peered at you to inquire or just to listen, he focused on you attentively. He towers over you, even now, in his 10th decade, fixing his gaze on you. Though it's a bit intimidating, it's still quite effective.

Next, the willing learner should demonstrate a facility picking up new languages needed to master a related clinical area. Knowing another language, even a symbolic language, as in mathematics or chemistry, opens up lines of communication and access to literature that broaden intellectual horizons. Most well-educated people will not be fluent in a foreign tongue, like Soma Weiss was. Yet, it is an essential role of a teacher and mentor to direct pupils toward languages; new means at exploring and accessing information.

Liberally educated individuals realize their intellectual freedom to admit that they do not know something. They develop the ability to discern which facts should be laid down in their brains as well-worn pathways and which facts are best left in books and computers as references. The rearrangement and manipulation of these facts [juggling] are what Stead refers to as 'thinking'.

Another key characteristic of the well-educated student is the acceptance of differences in peers. This acceptance, this tolerance by the 'Steadian' definition has a central nervous system component; it is not merely a conceptual ideal. There are certain irreversible brain characteristics that differentiate one student from the next. Thus, true acceptance is achieved when the instructor realizes that each student has limits to their capabilities; each will not reach the same height. Yet, the well-educated teacher can teach to all of them; even on ward rounds.

This neurologic basis for behavior differences means that love, hate, and other emotions, music, and the arts, are portions of the brain that are not easily measured by college examinations or in the clinic. But, Stead believed that the liberally educated student should appreciate the changes in the brain caused by socialization, culture, religious beliefs, history, and other aspects of one's culture. He or she should appreciate the complexity of socioeconomic problems. Even as far back as the Boston City Hospital days, Stead had noted the relationship between acute illness and poverty.

Whatever aspects of learning they are drawn to, to be truly well-educated, they must demonstrate an honest joy of learning and continue learning into old age. Dr. Stead noticed that many of the students he saw entering medical school appeared to have sought out few learning experiences purely out of personal desire; that is, doing things just because they wanted to.

" I don't want to influence anybody. I want to learn the doctor trade and make six thousand dollars a year. My boy, If you only knew how foolish you sound when you try to be cynical! When you are as old as I am, you'll understand that the glory of being a doctor is that you can teach folks high ideals while you soothe their tortured bodies."

None of the hectic activities of senior year-neurology and pediatrics, ...work in obstetrics, ...case histories..., attendance on operations, learning not to look embarrassed when charity patients called one "Doctor"-was quite so important as the discussion of "What shall we do after graduation?"

"I admit we should not be able to turn out doctors to cure village bellyaches. And ordinary physicians are admirable and all together necessary-perhaps. But there are too many of them already. And on the 'practical' side, you gif me twenty years of a school that is precise and cautious, and we shall cure diabetes, maybe tuberculosis and cancer, and all these arthritis things that the carpenters shake their heads at them and call them 'rheumatism.' So!"

from Arrowsmith by Sinclair Lewis, c1925, 1st ed., P.F. Collier, New York, pp. 15, 114, 128

Revolutionary Changes in the Curriculum

Some of the changes that Dr. Stead voiced to improve the medical school curriculum in the later years of his chairmanship in Durham were not all that popular with the administrative bodies. One of these was concerning the stated tuition charged and that undergraduate medical training extend for four full years. Stead believed these concerns were the greatest impediments to curriculum changes for the better. In his days as Dean at Emory, Stead had learned this basic tenet of university financing [see 'Afterword...' at the end of this volume].

Stead felt that a large amount of what the medical student was required to learn was useless. He would have rather deleted two years of learning useless material than to use these years wastefully. Better still, would be to replace this wasted time with useful experiences. Tuition costs could also be decreased. One can see how the P.A. programs are conceptually allied with this way of thinking.

Another constant impediment to curriculum change, more often than not, was the existing faculty. Frequently, the long-time faculty members would input knowledge in customary ways. Young, unspoiled learners would view facts in new ways and would generate new knowledge. They would achieve things in spite of the faculty.

Men are wise in proportion, not to their experience, but to their capacity for experience.   George Bernard Shaw[22]

Physicians of the Present

In April of 1971, the *Archives of Internal Medicine* [10,11] dedicated an issue to a great physician/educator/researcher who had been at Duke for many years. Dr. John Hickam was a long-time friend of Dr. Stead's who had been accompanying him in his medical odyssey since his days in Boston. John Hickam died while in his chairmanship at Indianapolis at age 56 from a ruptured cerebral blood vessel. He harbored the same malady as his chief from years previously at the Peter Bent Brigham

Hospital, Dr. Soma Weiss. On this somber occasion, Dr. Stead published an original article describing what he and his departed friend had discussed at length concerning the present and future of medical education.

Their discussions centered particularly around students and physicians-in-training. They believed medical and allied medical education needed to be broadened and should include other courses besides the basic sciences. Thus, sociology, economics, engineering, information sciences, and other areas should be included; not just chemistry, biology, physics, and mathematics. Those latter traditional courses support the easiest understood function of the physician, but such disciplines might limit the practitioners and the types of services they could offer the patient.

The traditionally trained physician is taught to subgroup the patients so that he or she can provide them with the best, most up-to-date information to manage the problem. The more precise the subgrouping, the more precise is the information and the better the assistance the practitioner can give to the patient, Stead explained. Some subgroup advice is patently obvious; like the kind you get on the evening news [avoid jogging where there are angry packs of rottweillers]. However, Stead was interested in providing young doctors with the skills to delineate definitive, complex subgroups, so that they could give people "special input"; they could educate patients about their particular disorders, teach them how to avoid factors which exacerbate their

177

difficulties, and help them enhance things which were advantageous to them.

To quote Dr. Stead in that presentation, "The medical drama has infinite variability, but its...form...[is] more fixed than the classical Greek play." Why shouldn't medical education have this same variability; our technology for diagnosing certainly does. Stead discovered that as our scientific methods became better at defining clinical problems; as we devised more means for analyzing disorders, we could improve medical management based on better subgrouping and further develop new areas of research. For example, now we can define a subgroup of diabetics that have certain amounts of protein in their urine-microalbuminuria. Our medical management of their difficulties may differ for those patients now that we can identify them. Yet, a lot of this process evolved out of not confining ourselves to the usual approaches and tests written down in the popular medical texts and literature.

The wise clinician uses many different, at times unconventional, frames of reference to determine the subgroup to which the patient belongs. He also realizes that abnormalities even abnormalities of behavior may have a structural or chemical basis in the body that we can not yet delineate with current methods. Stead went on to explain that bodies themselves have limits to positive changes we try to institute as practitioners. Improved methods point out the limitations of the body are less than we, the so-called educated providers, suspected; for example, neurons are more flexible than we thought; some cells regenerate faster than we estimated; genetic therapy is now available. The training grounds of physicians of the future, the universities, should be flexible also, like the body.

I envy no man who knows more than myself, but pity those who know less.   *Sir Thomas Brown*   *[22]*

Physicians of the Future, Perpetual Students of the Present

Choosing the optimum treatment for patients depends on proper subgrouping and the input of many non-primary care personnel: psychologists, chemists, nurses, physician assistants, pathologists, anatomists, and social workers. In addition, Dr. Stead sees no clear distinction between the physical sciences, the biological sciences, and the social sciences. Utilizing my literary license [akin to the poetic variety with no expiration date], this author feels there may be room for occasional humanities, and perhaps the arts, in this scheme.

Other clinical arenas are contributing to our understanding of subgroups. Computers were a welcome addition, recognized by Stead as an important means of handling, even rearranging the data explosion that one was witnessing in the '70s. With the technological advances that allowed tissue transplantation and pacemaker placement, patients could be moved into more treatable subgroups.

179

All these changes in the medical realm meant that medical education needed to keep pace; Dr. Stead saw it years ago. The data that students were learning in medical school, as well as in premedical preparation, proved less useful in the non-academic world, especially outside the hospital wards. Besides, in the practitioner's busy work day, there was little free time left to continue the lifelong educational process. Premedical, medical, and post-medical education needed more of the social sciences to create a broader 'managing physician', not just traditional doctors. Stead implored the medical education community to start producing physicians who could either practice medicine or help design and run healthcare systems.

Universal health care would be possible, according to Stead, only if some basic economic, social, and political issues were tackled first by health providers. From Drs. Stead's and Hickam's experience, a considerable amount of the premedical course requirement in basic science could be replaced with other course material to support the managerial development of the doctors of the future. Production of physicians knowledgeable in social and managerial sciences would require the following changes in the medical schools:

1. the development of outreach programs by universities into the community.
2. acceptance of new divisions on curriculum, admission, and promotion committees.
3. admission of a different type of student with academic strength in these alternative areas.
4. the agreement that no one department can determine that a student cannot be a doctor.

Both kinds of students, those interested in biosciences and on a non-traditional track, might be enrolled to the student body of the medical school. This model might also be a pattern for emerging nations, Stead continued. While Stead felt the bioscience model was good for educating physicians to give personal health service, he believed it was inadequate to aid in managing health care systems.

It is a distinct art to talk medicine in the language of the non-medical man.   *Edward H. Goodman [22]*

The Evolution of Medical Education

Prior to his article noted above at the symposium honoring Dr. Hickam, Stead had already proposed similar ideas in his article published in 1964 in *The Journal of Medical Education [13]*. In addition, he brings up related points. He notes that as the university has developed, the students, both graduate and undergraduates, have become more alike. This coincides with Stead's brand of teaching; teaching to various levels of medical trainees simultaneously. On ward rounds he would teach by the bedside to students, interns, residents, and colleagues. This notion also follows his history; during wartime, trainees would fill in for their clinical 'superiors' when the hospital was short-staffed.

On a more personal note, advancing through the complex medical education system myself, we were always taught procedures using the maxim; 'see one, do one, then, [the ultimate learning experience] teach one.' Everyone benefited from this hierarchical method, even the patient. It was classic 'Stead', even for my peers outside of Duke.

At about this time, the growth of the NIH helped establish many full-time faculty positions connected to clinical research. This led to the development of intramural programs to complement traditional medicine. For the first time health care became a real team effort, getting other areas to add new perspectives in solving patient problems. A multi-pronged approach to clinical problem solving became customary. The student body, as well as the faculty, evolved, containing those not previously viewed on the clinical scene; people with advanced training in psychology, sociology, engineering, and economics, all who intended to use their training in the medical field. No longer would these intelligent individuals have to abandon their studies or ideals to pursue a health-related career. The applicant pool to medical universities was getting more heterogeneous; the medical manpower and womanpower was bigger than ever; and it was changing its face.

> *Medical education [as]...a challenge can only be measured by the contribution...in the area of developing new models of medical care...and the distribution of this care to all citizens. ...[T]he university medical centre ...will acquire new knowledge...and scholarship.*
>
> *Moshe Prywes, Medical education and the nation's health, World Med. Jl., 16:87-95, 1969*

Stead and the Student Body

There are hoards of students in college that desire to be a doctor, but have a minimal interest in the basic sciences and are a bit puzzled that they are required to learn a lot of material which practicing physicians hardly ever use. Additionally, if you recall Stead's forgetting curve [remember?], the information you need may reside in that neuronal netherworld beneath the arachnoid space [above the brainstem]. Thank goodness for medical libraries and computers; not to mention ongoing research. Now, what did the accepted college graduate have to look forward to, according to Dr. Stead?

During the four years of medical school, there was a general survey of the medical field. Following this there might be three or more additional years of surveying. By the time all this surveying was over, Stead felt the trainee might be too old to learn. He or she may also have forgotten the reasons they had for desiring this prestigious career in the first place. The decision that also needed consideration at this point is, now armed with all this data and these credentials, does the graduate want to only pursue clinical care or acquire more scientific knowledge that leads to medical discoveries.

With the continued growth in the health care field, there are new departments and sections to be considered by the medical graduate and more information to introduce to the medical student. Yet, the curriculum was somewhat limited. Thus, Stead felt the final two years of medical school, should be elective time and students should have earlier contact with patient care; 'experiential' knowledge-what it's like to be a 'real doc'.

Stead made a distinction between a medical college, that provided students with the best current clinical information and a medical university, that emphasized a scholarly attitude in seeking out new knowledge for their students. Within the university, chiefs of clinical services had a dual responsibility for education and patient service. As he explained in his special article in 1963 in *The New England Journal of Medicine* [18], "...a teaching hospital is one in which intern and resident can teach.... Medical students are the greatest single asset of a teaching hospital." The student gives the intern and resident the precious commodity; 'time' to actively pursue learning, manipulate ideas, and, in turn, teach the student.

Stead also defined a non-teaching hospital and he considered some community hospitals too busy with other issues to provide excellent learning situations to students. He went on to delineate the advantages of having a VA hospital close to Duke Hospital staffed by the university physicians. In this setting, the student could be exposed to two essential types of learning. The first type Dr. Stead referred to as 'experiential'-patient care learning that includes understanding multiple variables; family setting, environment, behavior, and other social determinants. The second type of learning is related to the scientific, laboratory environment in which variables are controlled, yet can still be applied to clinical medicine. This dual nature of medical information is somewhat reminiscent of the teaching method used by Dr. Stead's mentor, Soma Weiss.

They do certainly give very strange and new-fangled names to diseases.   Plato   [22]

Producing Happy, Understanding Doctors

Patients have non-technical needs and the education of providers of healthcare starts way before medical school. Doctors-in-training need to demonstrate an ability to enjoy life through various brain inputs, such as literature, art, music, and drama, Stead believes. By using these alternative pathways, one hopefully discovers that the distinction between work and play blurs considerably.

Doctors should have both a reading and speaking knowledge of history, political science, government, economics, sociology, and religious thought which allows them to be effective citizens in this democracy as well as a good communicator with patients, according to Stead. The physician needs this broad educational base to be an effective communicator with persons from a wide variety of backgrounds. Still, the doctor needs to underlie this flexibility with an understanding of the biological basis for behavior. This proficiency is not obtained well by taking courses in the humanities, he feels; it's better taught as a part of bioscience.

To be well-rounded, Stead believes medical students "should be urged to explore the world around them...[and enjoy] a wide variety of areas." Personal enjoyment is as important as the economic security they seek. Then the 'word/pictures' they transmit to their patients to educate them will be more effective. If these pictures are worth a thousand words, as is touted, then word/pictures are probably worth more verbiage. This seems like a clear endorsement of the social sciences, as well as the biosciences, especially social anthropology.

The physician, thus, needs to be broadly educated, acceptant of many different lifestyles, and conscious of an individual's limitations. These limitations are based on the biological structure of the nervous system. Our ability to change behavior for health becomes harder as the patient ages; the plasticity of the brain is greater in the earlier years of life. To quote Stead, "All isn't lost after the age of seven...", though. There's still hope for us older individuals.

Experience is the great teacher; unfortunately, experience leaves mental scars, and scar tissue contracts. William J. Mayo [22]

The Tall Teacher and The Big Picture

Stead was an unusual teacher full of not-too-tall tales. He taught his students to question the medical knowledge that we all take for granted. He told us that no question is insignificant, especially if the answers have practical consequences for our patients. He grew up with a distrust of authority in many areas: art, morality, politics, and religion. He expressed the desire to examine institutions, as well as patients, critically [see 'Afterthought ...]. Stead was affected by the influences from the Edwardian Age; he described patient problems with the skill of a talented novelist.

His living novels were realistic; the stories were told with a purpose, rather than for a purpose; recollections of numerous patients that he had seen began in a social setting. Over the years, he became increasingly concerned with the social issues surrounding health care. The symposium honoring his retirement was comprised, in large part, of presentations of papers on providing health services. He predicted correctly that delivery of health care required a team approach, involving nurses, physician assistants, students of all kinds, nutritionists, social workers, and others. Proper applications of this personnel is still a challenge we face for the future.

Teaching should be contrasted with indoctrination. Indoctrination is a form of instruction which teaches certain tenets by precluding active inquiry which may question the validity of the so-called rules. Stead invited inquiry from his attentive audiences. Teachers are in a powerful position of authority for pupils are in no position to judge the truth or falsehood of what they are taught. Even Plato advised the guardians to teach the common citizens a 'noble lie' so that the people would blindly accept their station in life in his ideal republic. Stead, on the other hand, taught in less than an ideal, but close to ideal, university hospital in which students heard competing points of view; developing their abilities to dispute, question, and judge for themselves.

The doctor may also learn more about the illness from the way the patient tells the story than from the story itself.
James B. Herrick   *[22]*

Translation of Latin phrase: Experience will teach you many things.

10

Check; **Impressions**
by Robert Bloomfield, John Laszlo, Arthur Finn and others

The safest thing for a patient is to be in the hands of a man engaged in teaching medicine. In order to be a teacher of medicine, the doctor must always be a student.[22] Charles H. Mayo

ex priente lux, ex occidente lex

The White Cliffs of Dover are really off white, nowadays. The 'beautiful' Blue Danube is a slight shade of brown. My white coats are all a bit worn, now; they show the wrinkles of their underlying weave, though my red embroidered name is still quite legible, even in script. It's nothing that bleach and bluing wouldn't improve in my coat, or on the cliffs, or in the rolling river, for that matter; for the benefit of patients or the binocular-festooned tourists. Health-care has changed all over the globe. Managed care needs an urgent facelift, though reimbursement for a cosmetic procedure is not completely covered by most insurance carriers. Socialized medicine is barely presentable; lacking in several social graces. Technology is treading water in the cold Channel off of France. Healthcare has been floundering for years, looking up and down many coastlines for a safe harbor. I am always hoping not to go down with the ship in these imperfect healthcare storms. Patients should stay alert, waiting anxiously by the life boats.

We all really can learn a lot from Medicine's past; Hippocrates, Avicenna, Maimonides, Boerhaave, Harvey, Osler, and others. All these giants have lessons, questions, and stories; so does the present abridged life-story. The answers or morals from these lay, at times, hidden in fragments from various parts of the world; the East and West. We ought to listen more to them all and to the patients, at least, some of us. Listen more to Dr. Eugene Stead, whose motto might be subliminal, but aptly paraphrased from Descartes, "I think, therefore, I am gonna think some more".

You may not be as interested in what I think, having talked with, but not trained with Dr. Stead. I think that Stead imparted medical philosophy better than other teachers. Thus, I have also collected a few comments from colleagues who worked with Stead in the past. They, too, have stories to tell. Don't fall asleep, yet. It seems to be that when you are working on the reptilian portion of your brainstem, when all Betz [central nervous system cells] are off, when your convolutions quietly convalesce, inspiration seems to sprout; Dr. Stead seemed to believe that.

Considering Challenges with Dr. Stead

The first colleague of Dr. Stead's in this section, John Laszlo, was at Duke for many years and now lives in Atlanta, where he was Vice President of the American Cancer Society. He recapitulates Dr. Stead's colorful, variegated history. His manuscript, *The Doctor's Doctor [28]*, consisting of in-depth interviews with Dr. Stead, provided much information as a source for the present publication.

I remember sitting in the dentist's waiting room, reading about the most unforgettable character that that the writer had met. That came back to me in reflecting about the impact that Dr. Stead has made on many students, young doctors and colleagues. The dedication and intensity that we cherish in our favorite doctors is partly taught by their mentors in school and on the wards. That dedication to service may be why most of us went to medical school. But, how many of us come close to realizing our potential as the kind of physician, who can dissect out complex complaints, analyze the underlying physiology, and construct an optimal working plan to help patients?

Gene Stead was the doctor who helped other doctors to recognize their weaknesses and turn them into strengths. To be an intern or a resident on Dr. Stead's service meant being on call five nights out of seven. You were free every other week from noon Saturday until early Monday morning. This meant that the doctors lived in the hospital. The constant association with colleagues meant learning from each other. The many times of comparing notes at midnight 'supper', hearing about new admissions, listening again and again to interesting heart murmurs, and coming in the next morning to present to Dr. Stead. Working out the patients' problem and getting them into optimal health was the reward for all the work. Learning to take a social history on a poor black farmer with malignant hypertension enabled one to develop a realistic approach, often different than that in textbooks. The patient was the textbook and the problems were never the same, so the solutions varied accordingly. Dr. Stead rarely allowed students to talk about the textbook approach to patients. He wanted them to understand the pathophysiology of the illness and be able to explain it clearly to others. He then challenged the student to document his recommendations with the latest findings in the literature that applied to this patient, not just with the standard remedies.

My fascination with Dr. Stead was how this man, born to a very poor family could find his way through the rarified atmosphere of medical research and academia to become probably the pre-eminent Chairman of Medicine in the U. S. Young Stead was strongly influenced by his mother. Mrs. Stead worshiped at the alter of education and would attend college graduation ceremonies at nearby colleges. Gene was the first member of his family to go to college.

Enjoying the scholastic life, having straight 'A's but no special professional ambition of what to do beyond school was a problem that solved itself. Although not a pre-med., Gene knew he had to do something to make a living, and opportunities were scarce. Towards the end of his junior year he became involved in an argument with some chess-playing friends who were already in medical school. "I had never found anything very difficult at school ... I didn't go to medical school for any altruistic reason ...."

He would enter school in the fall of 1928 during the pre-Depression boll-weevil times, when the cotton crop was wiped out. The Atlanta Rotary Club that lent Stead tuition, continued to follow his progress. "It was expected that I would pay the money back, which I did ... [after] my education". Gene spent his time away from school and showed that he didn't have to spend as much time learning as others did. "I clearly frittered away the time. I don't know where the hours went but when it came to settling down and studying I could always pull it together". His dissection partner in Anatomy class tried to imitate Gene's work habits, but it didn't work for him and he flunked out.

During a clinical rotation at Grady Hospital, Gene was impressed with a very bright house officer. Inquiring where Dr. Wood had interned, Gene learned about the Peter Bent Brigham Hospital. That's where he set out to go, which began a 7-year stretch of being an impoverished house officer.

Not blessed with natural social graces and personally shy, his classmates wondered if he could be a success as a doctor. Gene found that while he couldn't meet patients socially he had no difficulty in caring for them. While impressed with his own medical ignorance, he found he could always do things for patients. He discovered that social graces and social skills are not always related. But since his experience at Grady was with taking care of many African-Americans, he wonders how he would have fared if he had been asked to care for white private patients. "The South was different then and nobody thought much about it. I was too busy trying to figure out how to eat to stay alive".

Before leaving Emory he noted that the Chairman of Medicine was not very effective, in part, because he was always traveling. "During that time I developed my conviction that staying at home at the hospital was the single most important ingredient to being a successful chairman. It's a whole lot more important than being brilliant."

One other Stead leadership principle was that authority cannot be given-but it can be taken. After his initial years of training in Boston, he went to the Cincinnati General Hospital to become Chief Resident. He lived in the hospital, as usual.

Medical students rotated through his service and often indicated that they wanted to intern at the Cincinnati General. But if Gene Stead did not think they were superior students he told them to go elsewhere to study medicine and that if they didn't, he would refuse to sign the certificate indicating they had passed senior medicine. "I took a great deal of responsibility for student teaching and supervised them closely." Stead changed the emphasis of teaching on the service from being based on what was known to what wasn't yet known about medicine.

Stead single-handedly integrated the medical service. The adult service was segregated into black and white, men and women. As a result there were always unused beds in some wards when there was no space for very sick patients in other wards. "I didn't like that idea of special areas restricted to a certain group so I set out to change it. I simply ordered the change based on expediency for patient care. The reaction to this integration was mixed. One of the virtues of the system though, was that unless Dr. Blankenhorn was on the ward, [Stead's] word ruled. Our new arrangement increased the workload for the house staff because they couldn't count on having any empty beds, but I must say I didn't really worry about what the staff thought. I was having a great time."

193

His leadership was greatly appreciated by his Chairman who thanked him for the changes he brought to the service. When he left, Blankenhorn gave Gene a photograph and an inscription that read "To Gene Stead, a Chief Resident in every sense of the word."

At times Gene Stead seemed ruthless in dealing with colleagues when he felt he was acting on behalf of service to patients. When he was at Emory as the chairman in the early days of World War II, he encountered a low quality medical program that was demoralized and short of full-time faculty.

Gene was surprised and delighted that 4 house officers from the Brigham volunteered to go to Atlanta to help him. They came for a salary of $400 per year and they all eventually became department chairmen. But the existing senior staff and house staff were not close to his standards and he wasted no time in making changes.

When Dr. Stead arrived at Grady, to his surprise he found a Chief of Medicine at the white Grady and one of the black Grady and neither had any intention of leaving. They were the only white doctors and the services were totally segregated. Not all of the doctors were Emory faculty members and most were not sympathetic to the medical school. Gene figured that since the two chiefs never spent more than an hour a day at the hospital and he would be there 18 hours a day, and since he had young doctors coming down from Boston to join him, he would take the authority and not worry about it. "So I simply started running the service. Some 18 months later the chiefs of both hospitals simply decided to resign.

And what about the house staff? "My first day at Emory I went to make rounds and found the Assistant Resident on the ward sitting at the nursing desk with his feet on the table, shirt open to his belly button, and a cigar in his mouth. He went straight into the army. I got there on the 20th of May and he was gone by July 1. ... I had decided that most of the residents at Grady Hospital who had been there when I came weren't going to do me any good, so I alerted the army that they might be expecting some more doctors. Just after the residents left for the army, Dr. Edward Miller arrived from Boston. I went to the ambulatory clinic at 9 AM one morning as usual to see 150 patients by myself when Ed came in. He took off his coat and that was his introduction to Grady Hospital. It was a long day as it was, but without people like Miller, Hickam, Beeson and Myers I never could have done it."

Of course Dr. Stead was a genius at medical diagnosis and developing treatment programs. To witness his command of history taking, physical examination, and ability to synthesize the facts of a case was to witness the art along with the science of medicine. The respect he received in this realm set him apart from all but a few people in American Medicine.

But his real genius was in recognizing research opportunities that others had missed and turning liabilities into assets. It took imagination, diligence, and a bit of what Gene calls 'free money' to invest in new ventures. Since he couldn't count on the Dean or Hospital Director or anyone to give him money to invest as he saw fit he had to find ways to start new projects without help.

So, what can you achieve academically in an impoverished, substandard city hospital, with inadequate staff and during wartime? And how can you build a reputation to attract good students, house officers and faculty?

Consider the tremendous number of cases of stabbing into the heart with ice picks that occurred every weekend at Grady. What an opportunity to study cardiac tamponade and cardiac repair. So you put a research team together that works every weekend around the clock. Or, how about getting an army contract to study plasma expanders, like albumin, which would be invaluable in combat zones? Or, how about competing for army money to set up a syphilis center to study the effects of a new antibiotic, penicillin, in a city with a large army base?

Getting hold of 'free money' to recruit outstanding faculty and initiate new projects really carried Dr. Stead in his years at Duke, especially the early years before grants began to flow. He put a substantial tax on the income of full-time faculty engaged in private practice... and they loved it! Why? Because it gave these physicians, who were higher paid than faculty engaged in research, a stake in the research accomplishments at Duke. They were real contributors and it justified their being at an academic institution.

Of course any who didn't wish to be taxed and wanted to make more money were encouraged to go elsewhere. You couldn't bargain with Dr. Stead. If a faculty person reported to him that he had a better offer, Gene would encourage that person to take it. He never wanted to pay his faculty so much money that they couldn't afford to leave Duke. The money saved was plowed back into the program and everyone understood this and most appreciated his frugality.

How was he so effective with his students and house officers? For one thing, he drove, not encouraged but drove, his students to perform at a level that was far beyond their own expectations. Decades later they will tell you that this experience was the highlight of their education. For those who internalized the lessons of how to learn from your patient in order to best serve, rose to the top of the field in their own growth. They had to present at the bedside, demonstrate physical findings, and then to discuss the case in the conference room. Woe to anyone who made up phony answers to questions posed by Dr. Stead or who tried to bluff The Chief! If the student didn't know the answer the intern would get a chance, then the resident. If no one knew, then they would be required to find out and be prepared on the next day of rounds.

Dr. Stead never forgot, no matter how hard people wished that he would! One illustration was with a former resident who came to visit 10 years later and Stead asked him about a chart on which he had left an incomplete piece of laboratory data as a resident. Details were important and they needed follow-up. Being overworked was never an excuse, for "the sick never inconvenience the well", as he would remind the supplicant.

It is often said that you can tell a 'Stead-trained' doctor by their approach to the philosophy, as well as the knowledge of medicine. How to get right to the nub of the problem, how to help the patient deal with the reality of their illness and do so in a sympathetic and uplifting fashion, how to communicate with families on their level of comprehension, these skills were learned at the bedside with Dr. Stead.

How could an important Chairman of Medicine take almost childish delight in a running discussion about a patient over the course of days and then having his student prove him wrong? It didn't happen often, but the students almost always rose to the challenge. They might even win a bet for a cherished nickel.

Most of the great chairmen of medicine I have known were not humble people who could feel joy in being proven wrong. Not that Gene was humble or modest about his skills. In

196

fact, he was so self-confident that he never feared being humiliated. He told me that he "would not walk across the street for fame", and he said this with the perspective that our personal accomplishments are not even tiny specks in geological time. The challenge was always to do the best possible job for the patient, and in so doing, the doctor learned, and so did Dr. Stead. He loved to learn and was grateful to those who could teach him. "If I had to be remembered for just one thing, I'd like it to be that I was an educator, and interested in the process of learning."

John Laszlo, M.D.
Former Professor of Medicine, Duke Univ. Medical Center
  National Vice President for Research, American Cancer
  Society (ret.), Atlanta, GA

I didn't meet Dr. Stead until shortly after I arrived in Durham in July of 1959. I was one of the Junior Assistant Residents (JARs) in Medicine. Dr. Stead attended regularly on Osler ward. His job was to appear at 10 a.m. three days a week, to teach until 12. His presence was felt by all of us at all times.

We worked 5 nights a week. One of the rules was that the order in which the patients were seen was sacrosanct: the student worked the patient up first, then the intern, and finally the JAR. As a consequence, I and my associates rarely finished seeing patients until well after midnight, and we sharpened our table tennis game, often from 2-4 a.m.

Dr. Stead reminded us that patients didn't like coming to hospitals, especially at 3 a.m. This helped me a good deal on those mornings when the phone rang in the wee hours just after I had fallen asleep, and it was the ER calling to tell me that my intern was seeing someone and was about to admit him/her. My first reaction was something like, "Darn, another patient to rob me of my sleep". However, I remembered Dr. Stead's comment, and realized that the patient was no happier to see me than I was to see him, and from then on I was able to be professional.

Months passed; the sense of 'ol daddy blue-eyes' was always there. His size was, if not overwhelming, surely imposing as he would loop his long arm over the curtain rod around the patient's bed, stare at us and ask just what it was that the patient needed most. Life was hard for the JAR, for the buck stopped with us; we had to know everything about the patient and about what to do, or at least to be prepared to do the right thing soon. Never, Dr. Stead said, would we ever know about patients until we saw them every day and night and got to understand them and their diseases.

With all of these hours of working, Dr. Stead said that learning was for everyone on the service. That meant that if a patient had heart disease, we had to call the cardiologist; if she had liver disease, we had to call the gastroenterologist, etc. This was the case even if, for instance, I had become an acknowledged expert in one or the other subspecialty, or if the problem was minor. The idea was that all possible specialists had to be involved because, if not, how would they learn? We had control of my ward, and in the Duke system there was no way that a specialist would take over the care of the patient, but nonetheless the specialists had to be called in.

Sometimes learning was difficult because sleeping was rare. One morning I was on rounds and apparently fell asleep standing up and leaning against a corridor wall. Suddenly I heard Dr. Stead's accented voice, calling "Art!, Art?" "Yes, Dr. Stead", said I. "Are you sleeping?" he said. "Yes", I said. And he asked "why?" My honest response was "I was up all night." "Life is hard", said Dr. Stead, "and you don't have to stay here if you don't want to." I am not sure that I ever even blinked in his presence for months after that!

One day a young diabetic entered the hospital, and she was assigned to a third-year medical student, Mike, rotating on the ward. He was not a very good student, but he worked hard, and didn't leave the floor until about 3 a.m. We made work rounds at 7 a.m., and, as luck would have it, poor Mike didn't get in until we had passed his patient and discussed our plans for her for the day.

Well, Mike presented the case to Dr. Stead at ward rounds, and, when the 'boss' asked him how much total insulin she had received since admission, he was off by 5 units (which she had received sometime after 4 a.m.) because he hadn't been to work rounds and hadn't had a chance to go over her chart. He then asked what her urine sugar had been that morning, and he didn't know that either, and for the same reason. Immediately Stead said "can you do serial sevens?" The student, quite alarmed, said that he could. Dr. Stead said "I don't think that you should pass third-year Medicine if you don't know how to work up a patient properly", and he walked out of the ward.

I chased after him and tried to persuade him that he wasn't being fair, that he intimidated the student, and didn't he, after all, notice that the student presented the case in a low voice while looking steadfastly at the floor. Dr. Stead replied that he thought he was being fair, and "Art, do I intimidate you?" Of course I responded that he didn't (ha!). He said that, in any case, fear was not an acceptable reason for not knowing about the patient. "Did you, Art, know the patient's total insulin dose and her a.m. sugar?" Well, of course I did. "Art, is he a good student?" Well, I had to admit that he wasn't very good, but that he worked hard, and that in any case I didn't feel that there was enough evidence from this one performance to fail him in Medicine. Dr. Stead disagreed, and required the student to repeat the rotation. In fact, I now think that he was more right than wrong, and I can only hope that eventually the student was better off (and certainly his patients were) by repeating Medicine.

When we rotated on the private service, the JARs spent an hour or so every morning in Dr. Stead's office, discussing whatever came to mind. He would sit there and make long chains from paper clips, sometimes pontificate, sometimes say nothing (and we had a game in which we tried to say nothing until he did; that was our mistake, because he could sit and remain totally quiet forever), but always when he did talk, managed to confound us. His circumlocutions were mixed well with little nuggets of knowledge, and his style was, well, different. I guess I learned from him in those sessions, mostly about caring and maybe even a few facts, but for the life of me I don't remember many specifics. An attachment grew, perhaps from wonderment about how such a man thought. He told us that knowledge of a disease was never complete until we had mulled it over for a long time. He likened it to the behavior of a child and a marble. The child, he would explain, would never really 'know' the marble and it would therefore never really become his until he had studied it from all sides, rolled it in every direction and distance, and done all of this for a long time. So, too, was the acquisition of all medical knowledge. We didn't 'own' it until we knew it from every angle.

He believed that no physician was competent until he or she 'knew himself', and to that end he wanted all of his chief residents to have extensive psychoanalysis. All did, except for Grace Kerby.

One of his unusual characteristics was that he tended to make up his mind about people rather quickly, and that once he did this he always stuck by that person. His choices sometimes were strange. I remember him carrying on about one member of the faculty who was obviously a pet of his. His name was Bill Lynn, and he was a physician and biochemist with some crazy, and occasionally creative, ideas. It was for this that Dr. Stead loved him. One day he defended him by saying something like "this man is such an original thinker that he could look up at a fluorescent light and work out its biochemistry and then want to study the effects of fluorescent lighting on the behavior of patients with this disease or that", or something equally unorthodox. His point was that Dr. Lynn was so very creative and clever.

He reminded us regularly that even if we were not as clever as Bill Lynn was, we could and we would learn about patients and about diseases, and also teach. Teaching was a very big deal, as indicated in part by the requirement already mentioned that consultants had to be called. However, their role was absolutely specific: they were required to talk to the intern before writing even a single word in the chart. Nothing like that happens at UNC; consultants see patients, then write notes (with recommendations for therapy etc.) and don't make it a habit of seeking out the intern who requested the consultation. That simply was unacceptable at Duke, and, as far as I knew, never happened. I also spent a year as a Senior Assistant Resident (SAR), and it was to that person that the role of writing consultation notes fell. S/he made rounds with his/her consulting attending, and a decision was made about diagnosis and therapy. The SAR would then do things in the right order, and this would fulfill the teaching role for the SAR. With all of this, it was equally clear that Dr. Stead's overwhelming concern was for the patients.

With all this, and 5 nights a week besides, what was that year like? Hell, maybe, but all of us had, or developed, this incredible fealty toward Dr. Stead. It was some kind of mass hypnosis, I think, but we died a million deaths during the year, and loved Dr. Stead for making it happen. Several years ago, following the unfortunate death of a teenager in New York, presumably due to misdiagnosis and delayed treatment of meningitis by an overworked and overtired medical house staff, a hue and cry went up, and was assuaged, to insist that residents must work shorter hours. Again recently the same pronouncement was made, and again presumably for the same reasons: overtired house staff might mistreat patients. Dr. Stead's pronouncement that there was no way to learn about disease other than by seeing patients is now falling on deaf ears. We were overworked but never overtired. I believe that patients are going to suffer in the long run because internists are simply not going to be knowledgeable enough to care for them the way we learned to. Perhaps there is some intermediate time schedule between five of seven nights and 1 in 5, but the latter is simply short-changing the house staff and, eventually, the patients.

Did we ever make mistakes on Dr. Stead's service? I honestly don't think so. I think that we were in better shape, that patient care was less complicated, and the system just didn't allow that to happen because every move of every student was watched over by the intern, his/hers by the JAR, and his/hers by Dr. Stead and the ever-present Dr. Grace Kerby, whose permanent presence on the wards provided her with total familiarity with every patient and every note on every chart. There was just no room for errors; there simply wasn't. Dr. Stead simply willed it so.

I took two years as a post-doctoral fellow with Louis G. Welt in Chapel Hill, and became a nephrologist. I then returned as an SAR with Dr. Stead. That year was easier, but the rules hadn't changed, and, I became a teacher instead of a ward leader.

I left Duke in June of 1963 and went to the NIH for two years as a Visiting Scientist. Somewhere around the middle of my first year I got a call from Dr. Stead offering me the job as his chief resident the following year. He said that I should talk to my wife, Debbie, that he would pay me $9,500, and that I should call him the next day at 2 p.m. with my decision. I was shocked and flattered and had the presence of mind to ask him whether he would still love me even if I were to decline his offer. He of course assured me that he would.

I was in a state of panic. I loved the science I was learning and doing, and I had a promised position on the faculty at UNC as soon as I left the NIH. I would start as an Assistant Professor of Medicine, and would be able to do science and be a clinician;

why did I need to go back to Duke? Well, it was already known by the medical world that this was a plum job, and that many of Dr. Stead's chief residents had risen to be chairmen of Departments of Medicine. I asked everyone I knew, including my bosses at the NIH. After a while I decided that even though I would get to meet Bingham Dai for psychoanalysis, I really didn't want the job.

And so, the following afternoon at the appointed hour, I called Dr. Stead and told him that I would like to become a member of a very exalted society, and one with few members, namely the society of those who had turned him down for this job. He seemed to take it well.

Several years later, I finally returned to Chapel Hill after a 5-year stint on the faculty at Yale. By this time, Dr. Stead had appointed one of his ex-house officers, Ike (Roscoe R.) Robinson as head of nephrology.

What did Dr. Stead leave for me? I have mixed memories and feelings, but consider him to have been a phenomenon unlike any other I have ever met. I don't think I could write this much about anyone else not related to me, and I guess that he had the greatest impact on me of anyone I have ever met. On the other hand, I could never call him a role model, for I couldn't possible be like him even if I wanted to. One needs to meet such a person perhaps only to fill gaps in one's experiences. He surely filled many of mine, and I guess I will carry this view of him forever: a thoughtful, strong, brilliant and articulate man who, though occasionally wrong, was never in doubt and could never lose a debate simply because those of us on the other side could never understand enough about what he was saying to argue with him decisively.

Arthur Finn, M.D., Professor of Medicine and Physiology, UNC-Chapel Hill, North Carolina

Before I met Dr. Eugene Stead, I had known him by reputation-as a distinguished internist, esteemed academician, and medical scholar. ...I served with him at the National Library of Medicine [NLM] Board of Regents, I found that he was ... a gentleman, an interesting conversationalist, and a kind and modest human being. His contributions to discussions at the ... board meetings were always pertinent, well-reasoned, and clearly expressed. When ... seeking eminent physicians ... [with] inspiring medical careers ... Dr. Stead ... represents the highest ideals of his profession and is truly an eminent American physician.

(edited) Dr. Lois DeBakey, Baylor College of Medicine
Houston, Texas, June, 2000   [15]

Understanding Dr. Stead's Retirement

[When] Dr. Stead told me he was soon to retire, ... [of] course I asked, "Why?"... [He] replied, "To run a good department, one has to take risks and make changes that should advance the department but [these] might not materialize as well as planned and [this could] have a serious adverse effect on the department. When you are in your early fifties ... you have a lot of years ahead [of you] .... If the potentially riskful change resulted in adverse events, you['d] have adequate [remaining] years in which to work and develop an even stronger department. ...if you and your colleagues know you are going to retire at 60, [then] if a change you introduced in your late 50s did not do well, the department would know that. [The department would be aware and], if by your youthful vigor, you could not correct the problems, you would soon be gone. ...[But], if you experienced bad results ..., when you were in your early 60s, you'd have less vigor with which to correct adversities; yet, you would be around until 70." As he was approaching 60 and the department was [still] going strong, he was going to 'step down'.

Henry D. McIntosh, M.D., M.A.C.C.
Former Chairman of Medicine,
Baylor College of Med., Houston
Former Prof. of Med., DUMC
Durham, NC

Translation of Latin phrase:
Light comes out of the East, law from the West.

Considering Challenges with Dr. Stead

11

Adapting strategies; **Healthcare Crises and Medical Education in the U.S. and in Developing Nations**
by Dr. B. Lown and a note by Dr. H. McIntosh, edited and supplemented by Dr. R. Bloomfield assisted by Dr. Pedley

Three passions, simple but overwhelmingly strong, have governed my life: the longing for love, the search for knowledge, and unbearable pity for the suffering of mankind.
Bertrand Russell

leve fit quod bene fertur onus

Each of the contributors to this portion of this volume has also contributed to society at large. They are not likely to expound on their many accomplishments. While Eugene Stead promoted his perspectives locally and nationally, two of his compatriots share his energetic vision on an international level.

I appreciate, first, the input of the inventor of the DC defibrillator and recipient of a Nobel Peace Prize, Dr. Lown, for his initial rendering for this chapter. Next, Dr. McIntosh has used his technological understanding to establish an effective endeavor to distribute cardiac pacemakers to foreign, infirmed, often indigent individuals in need in distant cultures. References from each of these authors are listed at the end of this chapter. Both are accomplished in their own fields; but, perhaps more importantly, they have each applied their medical knowledge to promote a precious gift-world peace.

What follows is a summary from several relevant publications and my own personal communications with these two accomplished individuals. Pertinent references [some marked with lower case letters] are listed in the final bibliography at the conclusion of this volume; others are noted at the end of this chapter. Personally, they have both had experiences with Dr. Eugene Stead over many years and, although these writings embody their own personal philosophies, their works support the legacy of Dr. Stead. Legacies are composed of the works of great thinkers-Holmes, Osler, Levine, Stead, and others. The application of their thoughts include patient problems as well as broader cultural challenges. Concepts are passed down through the ages, not limited by personal contact.

Dr. McIntosh was a long-time associate of Stead's at DUMC. He and Eugene Stead shared many thoughts and experiences as they worked together. Dr. Lown's philosophy of teaching, on the other hand, embodies many of the main elements of Stead's concepts from a distance. It is not merely by chance, however, that Drs. Lown and Stead both studied under the same mentor in Boston, Dr. Sam Levine.

Dr. Lown speaks first of cardiovascular training:

Developing a World Cardiovascular Fellowship

We have reached a crossroads; residencies and fellowships need drastic restructuring. Shakespeare said, "New occasions teach new duties. Time makes ancient good uncouth." Before turning to the "new occasions" we need to reexamine the "ancient good."

The Lown Cardiovascular Group in Boston in affiliation with Harvard's Brigham and Women's Hospital has sustained a postdoctoral fellowship for more than four decades; an important achievement. Training doctors has been a key component of our mission which emphasizes the centrality of the patient. Any mission worth permanence needs disciples who master the essentials and disseminate the teaching.

No longer are we merely a family, we can lay claim to being a small and influential tribe. Our associates, students, residents, and fellows seed our philosophy to all continents and assure passing on our ideas to future generations.

Our own fellowship program was launched in 1957 in the hospitable environment of the Harvard School of Public Health. Philosophic inspiration stemmed from the great teacher at the Peter Bent Brigham Hospital, Dr. Samuel A. Levine [see chapter 3]. Back then he warned against a battery of technologies superceding a mind willing to think.

The curriculum we have devised aims to communicate our unique style and excite a reverence for the art of doctoring. First, we had to reeducate trainees and teach them that medicine is not merely a scientific discipline; employing appropriate technologies does not make many medical problems diagnosable and ultimately curable. Indeed, the practice of medicine, though dependent on scientific discoveries, is not purely a science. Each human being is marked by a measure of uniqueness and is replete with unpredictabilities.

No scientific algorithm, no formula enables easy deciphering of the individual hieroglyphic. Doctors have learned that to heal a patient requires time while participating in attentive and sympathetic listening (a). This is in effect the art of medicine, an exercise that connects patient and doctor in a healing relationship.

207

The curriculum aims to impart an holistic approach. Proficiency in the latest technology is not enough. The changes brought about by the onrush of scientific discovery makes all current approaches conditional and temporary. Solely mastering current technologies is a prescription for rapid obsolescence.

We shift the center of study away from the hospital, for the majority of problems are neither acute nor emergencies. If a deeper aim of doctoring is to prevent rather than cure disease, then a more balanced perspective is obtained by centering training within an outpatient clinic [see chapters 2 and 4]. Furthermore, we eschew being smitten by the latest miracle breakthroughs, emphasizing that good practice has to be evidence-based, derived from properly conducted randomized and, where possible, blinded studies.

Finally, when dealing with clinical problems, where variables are myriad and evidence favoring one course or another is often gossamer, required is a measure of common sense guided by well-leavened medical experience. The problem is when the resident or fellow is young and impressionable, common sense is not a strong suit and experience is meager. We resolve this dilemma through an mentoring relationship. Connecting intellectually with a seasoned clinician facilitates an osmosis of experience. We cultivate a close one on one relationship between accomplished physician and doctors in training. Ultimately, medicine is a moral enterprise, not easily taught, but insinuated by setting a good example.

adapted from *The Lown Forum* [b]
[with permission]

Medicine is based not only on science but on keen insights of brilliant teachers who have been able to assimilate a wealth of clinical experience and distill essential, widely generalizable conclusions. Bernard Lown, M.D.;

From: www.ProCOR.com

American Health Care in Crisis

US ranks 12th out of 13 countries based on 16 health indicators. This backwardness exists despite health expenditures twice that of other industrialized countries and exceeding one trillion dollars annually. The indicators are derived from such factors as life expectancy, child survival to age five, from out-of-pocket health expenditures and from a number of other factors which define high quality care (c). This inadequate performance was recently corroborated by the World Health Organization which ranked the USA 37th among 191 countries (d). A substantial reason for the poor outcome relates to the 44 million uninsured Americans. This is a national badge of shame, especially as it is occurring during a period of economic prosperity.

Another indicator of the dysfunctional medical system in the U. S. is the high level of dissatisfaction among health professionals. Doctors are made to feel like hamsters on a treadmill, running faster, but failing to progress (e). Health practitioners are inundated with a glut of paper work, responding to Draconian measures to enhance efficiency and profitability. Though well-established that spending more time with patients is effective in improving health care (f), the time permitted for professional interaction is continuously abbreviated. Nurses are brimming with outrage at staff cutbacks, increased patient loads, and demoralizing work conditions (g). The lack of professional satisfaction leads to early burn out. Applications to medical school are falling while the shortage of nurses is reaching crisis proportions. Health care increasingly resembles an industrialized process, with doctors working the assembly line and patients reduced to depersonalized commodities to be traded among insurance vendors.

To date, the essential strategy evolved in the wealthier countries has been curative rather than preventive. It has involved prodigious capital investment in high technologies managed by intensely trained super-specialists. This strategy has proved far too costly even for the U. S. with 70 per cent of physicians in specialties and with health expenditures equivalent to 14 percent of the gross national product (GNP) or about a $1 trillion annually. Despite the mammoth outlay, many people are totally bereft of health insurance and others have coverage limited only to catastrophic illness. The U. S. currently is aggressively attempting to diminish health care spending by curtailing physician autonomy in patient management. In fact, the richest country in the world can not afford a technology-based solution for cardiovascular and other disease.

The public, angered at being short-shrifted by impersonal health care, is turning in droves to alternative medicine, to self-medicating with food supplements, to consuming billions of dollars worth of untested herbal potions and even resorting to quack practitioners. The move away from scientific doctoring is also propelled by a growing realization that the present health care system is hazardous. Spending less time with patients leads to more referrals to specialists and more prescribing of drugs. The result is polypharmacy with inevitable adverse reactions and overindulgence in costly and risky invasive procedures. This view has been recently confirmed by the Institute of Medicine at the National Academy of Sciences. In an intensive study of health care quality in the U. S., a key conclusion was that fatal mistakes from the misuse of the medical technologies and potent pharmaceuticals now available are a substantial cause of death and disability. These harmful effects constitute the third cause of death in the U. S. and are responsible for about 400,000 fatalities annually, claiming more lives than tobacco, stroke, diet, alcohol, addictive drugs, firearms, or automobiles, behind only heart disease and cancer (c).

The pressure on expenditures is driven by an aging population with a growing burden of chronic disease, as well as by the introduction of even more novel technologies and costlier pharmaceuticals to cope. The health crisis is further stoked by floods of hype, surfeiting patients with high expectations of miracles which will annul suffering and death. Ignored is a more realistic policy keyed to educating the public on healthy life styles, and to allocating adequate social resources for communities to promote practices conducive to health.

There is a different path for mitigating the current health care crisis. This is based on investing much time with each patient, on practicing the art while cultivating the science and by resorting to technologies when benefit far outweighs hazard and cost. For example, of the many coronary patients who come to our group for second opinions relating to a costly intervention, we refer only about 15 percent for some invasive procedure. The outcome in patients managed conservatively with medical and

210

preventive strategies is as good as the best reported anywhere. In fact, a relaxed visit, a comprehensive history and thorough physical examination permits the doctor to sort out what is truly troubling the patient without the need to enfilade him or her with a multitude of drugs or referral to diverse specialists, each offering an array of costly and, at times, invasive technologies. As a result, our patients are less burdened with polypharmacy, are subjected to fewer procedures, and require fewer hospitalizations.

The Poorer Developing Nations

We live in an age of globalization accompanied by the melting away of national frontiers. More than 2 million people traverse across national boundaries daily. This leads to new risks in health that cannot be attended by each nation individually. It commands a global vision. In addition, there is a moral imperative to mitigate suffering wherever it is encountered. Nowhere is the problem as acute as in the developing world.

Poverty is the leading cause of poor health across the globe (h,i). Nine hundred years ago, Al Asuli, the great physician of Islam, living in what is now Kazakhstan, wrote a medical pharmacopoeia. He divided this treatise into two parts: "diseases of the rich" and "diseases of the poor." The passage of many centuries has not made the dichotomy obsolete; the divide between rich and poor is widening, both within industrialized nations, but more so between developing and developed countries.

In this age of potential abundance, more go hungry than ever before. Oxfam reports that one third of people in Asia, Africa, Latin America and the Caribbean are too malnourished to lead fully productive lives (j). Disparities between rich and poor nations are prodigious. The industrialized countries, with 21 percent of the world's population, account for 85% of the gross national product, of world trade, and of energy consumption. The poorest quintile contribute a meager 1.4% to the global gross national product and engage in only 0.9% of world trade (k).

This divide continues to grow. According to the UN, from 1960 to 1990 the per capita income increased four-fold among poor nations while registering an eight-fold rise among the wealthy ones. The difference in annual income is now more than 60-fold (l). The policies of structural adjustment, imposed on developing countries by the World Bank and the IMF, have emphasized debt repayment based on maximizing exports at the expense of agricultural self-sufficiency and social programs. These economic strictures have curtailed the already small funding for health services, education and the environment.

Absence of safe water, rudimentary sanitation, inadequate nutrition, lack of housing, faulty basic education and meager incomes [commonly less than one dollar a day], contribute to a foreshortened life span, as well as acute and chronic ill health. The major scourges are infectious disease, malnutrition, and reproductive hazards. In Africa, as in other regions of the poor world, there is a disparity between a mammoth disease burden and the small numbers of trained physicians. Many African countries have far less than one physician per 10,000 people. By contrast, in industrialized countries one physician is available for less than 400 people.

The low status of women is an additional contributor to morbidity and premature death. Endless drudgery, early marriage, teenage pregnancy, high fertility, inadequate nutrition, anemia and chronic infections are some of the risk factors accounting for the inordinate child bearing mortality. Harrison (m) has documented that fatality in pregnancy relates to women's status and is reflected by their level of education. A woman in Sierra Leone has one in 7 chances of dying as a direct result of pregnancy; in Britain, it is one in 6,000 (n).

The Cardiovascular Disease Epidemic

While unable to shake the disease of poverty, chronic degenerative ailments, generally associated with affluent societies, constitute a major cause of death in impoverished countries. In 1990, for example, two thirds of the 14 million cardiovascular disease [CVD] fatalities worldwide occurred in developing nations (o,p). In 1990 the proportion of CVD deaths occurring below the age of 70 years was 26.5% in rich countries as compared to 46.7% in poor countries (o).

One important factor for increases in CVD is the rising life expectancy, rapid and chaotic urbanization with accompanying life style changes, and powerful economic and cultural influences of globalization (q). The shift in agricultural production from small farmer to large corporation, distribution from shopkeeper to supermarket, consumption from fresh to processed foods, promote drastic changes in nutrition. Consumption of fat and salt increases and that of micronutrients diminishes. Calorie intake multiplies while physical activity lessens. The mismatch between energy consumption and energy expenditure manifests itself as a pandemic of obesity (r). Crowding, mass unemployment and wanton violence engender social and psychological stresses which are additional risk factors for CVD and diabetes. When one adds the rising consumption of tobacco products to these, the outcome is tragic. It has been demonstrated that good health care can be achieved in economically deprived nations without resorting to costly technologies (s). For example, poor countries like China, Jamaica and Kerala (province of India) with low GNP's have reasonably good health indices, such as life expectancy, comparable to those of developed countries. Another striking example is Cuba, tightly blockaded against the import of high technology, and with a GNP per capita approximately one twentieth of the U. S.; nevertheless with health outcomes not dissimilar to the rich colossus in the more northern latitudes. It is evident that poor countries do not have to invest in costly medical technology in order to promote good health and wholesome life expectancy for their people.

Currently, health care facilities are being privatized in several developing nations. In cities of developing countries, one can already witness new hospitals, fully stocked with cutting edge technologies to service the elite. These investments consume large chunks of health budgets at a time when funds are in short supply to deal with basic public health problems, such as safe drinking water. In a perceptive article written a decade ago, Woolhandler, et. al. (t) conclude that the problem has less to do with a moral failing of the developing world than with the irresistible pressure of a global system of economics, knowledge and techniques that foster inappropriate technology.

Woolhandler, et. al. (t) asks, "Can we continue to produce miracles for the few that are off-limits to the many?" Besides the immoral aspect of treating some people as of lesser worth, based on affluence, such an approach is economically untenable. In fact, when technology and advanced procedures are not available at home, people will seek it abroad; it is impossible to prevent citizens from gaining the latest in health care elsewhere.

A transfer of wealth from poor to rich countries is being cycled through the purchase of health care abroad. This is evident in Houston, Texas, where palatial sky-scraper hospitals have been built from fees of patients coming from all over Latin America. It may be more economic to construct a tertiary care hospital in a developing country than squandering scarce hard currencies abroad to provide medical services otherwise unobtainable. For example, a coronary bypass operation can be performed equally well in New Delhi as in New York, but at one tenth the expenditure [see chapter 4]. For the cost of a single bone marrow transplant done in Zurich or London, five could have been carried out in Zagreb (t).

[As established, somewhat privileged healthcare providers, we assume that our system of healthcare is worth exporting *in toto*. Dr. Lown advises us otherwise. Dr. Stead understood that each student he taught had their own particular strengths and weaknesses. Transfers of healthcare systems need to take this notion into account, applying it to individual cultures-ed.]

Some medical procedures have not been fully studied, yet many are used excessively, [e.g. pacemakers, endoscopy, cesarean sections, fetal monitoring, etc.]; procedures that we take for granted.

If evidence-based medical standards were to be applied to technology assessment, the cost problem facing developing countries would be significantly reduced. This challenge needs to be addressed.

Science and technology present a possible promise regarding a way out from poverty; however, one cannot invoke much optimism on that score alone. In the decade of the 70's, the increase in the number of scientists per one million of population was 637 in the industrialized countries contrasted with 42 scientists, or less than one tenth, in the developing world (u).

How will impoverished countries deal with the health challenges when resources for the public sector are scarce and diminishing? (v). Many developing countries are emulating our misdirected concentration on technologic measures rather than committing to sound public health policies; identification of susceptible populations and promoting healthy life styles with an emphasis on prevention. Scanty societal resources are being allocated to building tertiary care hospitals for the elite, while not pursuing the 'unfinished agenda' of infectious and nutritional disorders which almost exclusively afflict the poor masses (w).

Rational uses of technology can lead to substantial saving of health expenditures. Recent study demonstrates that containing risk factors for heart disease can halt or even reverse the very process of coronary artery narrowing. Controlling blood pressure or diabetes can be achieved at a small fraction of the expenditure required to manage their various complications. Educating and involving the community in health care decisions is essential if sound policies for the rational acquisition of medical technologies are to gain political support.

Health Information Poverty

If he has knowledge, what does he lack? If he has no knowledge, what does he possess?　　　*The Talmud*

The internet presents promising new vistas for democracy, education, and personal enrichment. Nothing in history has provided a potential for making readily available more information for more people at lower cost.

As with Al-Asuli's pharmacopeia, the divide between rich and poor applies to the sphere of health information as well. The industrialized nations are awash with new information technologies transforming the way health care is delivered. At the same time, three quarters of the world's population are starved for the most basic nutrients of the mind. Of Africa's 700 million people, only 800 thousand to a million, or 0.14%, are users of Internet services.

Information poverty is a substantial impediment to better health in poor countries. Inadequate fiscal resources have a direct impact on the availability of health information services. While a medical library in the U. S. subscribes to around 5000 journals, the Nairobi University Medical School Library, long regarded as a flagship center for medical literature, receives only 20 journal titles today compared to 300 the library subscribed to a decade ago (x). A recent visit to a district hospital in Brazzaville, served by 20 doctors, found a library consisting of a single bookshelf. The condition of the University hospital is not much better with only 40 old books and a dozen out-of-date medical journals (y). In the 1960s the Albert Cook Medical Library at Makerere in Kampala, Uganda boasted over 2,500 medical volumes and journal subscriptions, one of the largest; today it receives fewer than 40 medical journals. Not only are the journals in medical libraries few, they are torn and dated (z). A number of libraries have received no new books over the past decade, have no computer, have no access to databases and have no money for stamps to write for material (aa). A major reason for this has been ascribed to the failure of parent bodies or institutions to finance libraries (z).

As the information highway is privatized and commercialized, cost limits access. It is estimated that two thirds of all personal computers are bought by those with annual incomes of $40,000 or more in the U. S. (bb). The problem is a whole order of magnitude greater for poor countries. In the major cities of Africa, direct, real-time access to internet lines is obtainable through a growing number of internet service providers. However, hook up, access fees, and training costs are financially out of reach for a majority of health professionals. While the affluent travel at ever greater speed on the information highway, a majority of the world's population has never even made a telephone call.

... we should respect and help our nonscientific healers because in a large part of our daily practice, we are using nonscientific methods just as they do.   Eugene Stead, M.D.,

from *[26] What This Patient Needs is a Doctor, p60.*

SatelLife

SatelLife, founded in 1987 by Dr. Lown, has focused on delivering critical information where it is most needed. Satelife's electronic network, was initially based on low earth orbit satellite (LEO) technology, providing cost-effective and reliable technology for reaching remote areas of the world with inadequate telecommunication infrastructures. The LEO satellites were launched in 1991 and 1993 by the European space agency.

Each satellite, circles the earth four times daily, circumnavigating the globe in 100 minutes. As telephone lines have improved, health information can be moved more quickly and efficiently using standard telephone dial-up networks, and high-speed modems. Thus, over 95% of health information flows over telephone lines. However, the LEO satellite remains indispensable to communicate with a number of remote sites lacking adequate telephone services.

This combined network now serves approximately 4,000 health professionals in 25 countries. Through e-mail, electronic conferencing, and electronic publications, this entire network [HealthNet] has become a critical link for many on the front lines of the major public health battles being waged in poor countries.

Electronic publications such as weekly health news, provide current abstracts from leading peer-reviewed medical journals as well as full text articles. These are selected, based on their sound science and their relevance to a country's health problems. Royalty-free arrangements with 18 leading medical journals afford a wide range of communications. special software, relying on simple e-mail, enables practitioners to engage in electronic searches of 21 abstract data bases at the National Library of Medicine in Washington and receive relevant abstracts.

Promoting Awareness About the Cardiovascular Epidemic

The rich experience of the industrialized world, concerning their long history of coping with CVD, needs to be shared with the 'Third World'. A wealth of epidemiological observations point to the role of risk factors which can be modified by public health policies and life style changes (cc,dd). These lessons are especially pertinent in relation to the role of tobacco consumption now gaining a substantial foothold in poor countries. Available health information obviates the need to reinvent proverbial wheels. However, medical journals in the rich countries mirror their own health care practices.

Unsifted information from these ethnocentric sources could further distort the already strong tendencies away from population-based health policies. There are many medical journals already on the world wide web; needed is new information that is closely tuned to the health problems of poor countries. Such tuning requires a partnership of equals between health professionals of the many nations covering the entire developmental spectrum. The goal would be the sharing of information that is scientifically sound, reliable, pertinent, as well as affordable.

The challenge is to bring reliable information to the internet. This is essential for poor countries as they enter the global dialogue. Wiring the poor world, however, will not close the information gap between the 'haves' and 'havenots'. Improving information access will require a far more equitable global world order.

Four years ago, I launched a new web site with the assistance of two post-doctoral fellows, both from developing countries, Dr. S. Jabbour from Syria and Dr. M. Luna from Guatemala. Designated 'ProCOR', the objective was to create a platform for dialogue and for exchange of knowledge that focused on cardiovascular health in developing countries and thereby, to serve the needs of those on the front lines of the growing disease epidemics.

Merely being a conduit of information is insufficient in addressing the large and growing challenges to non-communicable disease. To succeed requires educating and empowering people to pursue healthy life styles, as well as implementing public health measures that attenuate risk factors at the community level. For this reason ProCOR has supported the organization of regional groups composed of health professionals and community leaders to promote public health education. These regional groups encourage health professionals of developing countries to participate in shaping the global agenda, as well as tuning the local program to the distinctive cultural and social needs of their particular country.

Physicians in affluent countries have a moral responsibility to work for global equity in health care. They bring a rich experience in coping with their own profiles of non-communicable disease. Two medical strategies have evolved over the past half-century (ee). One concentrates on the disease to be treated with advanced technologies administered by highly trained super-specialists. The other is focused on controlling the risk factors which lead to disease. There is now an abundance of data supporting the effectiveness of the preventive approach in reducing the burden of cardiovascular disease [CVD]. It is the major reason for the striking decrease in CVD mortality in industrialized countries. In the period of 1965-1990, CVD-related mortality fell by about 50% in Australia, Canada, France and the U.S. and by 60% in Japan (ff).

Effective training programs for cardiologists, especially those from poor, developing countries, will require an educational paradigm shift. The Lown Cardiovascular Group is adapting a novel program to meet the challenge. While instructing with the style of health care practiced by our group is an one element of the new curriculum, the trainees need to acquire a number of public health tools. In addition to partaking of classic medical subjects, they would have to gain proficiency in an array of new disciplines; among these epidemiology, nutrition, biostatistics, cost-effectiveness analyses, informatics, medical technology assessment, socio-economic determinants of health; and such unique areas as the utilization of mass communication to affect individual behavior as well as reshape cultural norms relating to health. Such a curriculum to be responsive to the problems confronting poor countries needs to shift emphasis from mastering procedures to learning how to control the diverse risk factors for disease (ff0).

Additional Thoughts

Those who live in affluence deplore the situation, but turn away from the moral challenge. As Tolstoy complained about the state of dispossessed serfs in Russia more than a century ago, "I sit on a man's back, choking him and making him carry me, and yet assure myself and others that I am very sorry for him and wish to ease his lot by all possible means-except by getting off his back." (ff1). The annual servicing of Africa's debt of $300 billion exceeds the funds available for health and education combined. An AIDS afflicted country like Uganda spends $2.50 per person per year for health and $15 on debt servicing (gg). Cancellation of at least part of this colossal debt from poor to rich countries [perhaps, tied to conditions of certain health-related reforms-ed.] would do more for improving health care than providing free subscriptions to leading medical journals for every health professional in developing countries.
[hh,ii]

B. Lown, M.D., Professor Emeritus of Med.,
Harvard, Chief Cardiologist, The Lown
Cardiovascular Clinic, Boston

A Note from Dr. McIntosh

[Dr. Lown is using his expertise to help healthcare globally. Meanwhile Dr. McIntosh, another notable cardiologist and protegé of Eugene Stead's, is attacking these international problems using a different approach, yet retaining a similar global vision.]

An old Kenyan proverb implores us:

Be kind to the earth.
It was not given to you by your parents....
It was loaned to you by your children.

There are billions of people on this 'fate-sharing ship...planet Earth.' If one is to be kind to this earth, the inhabitants must learn to live together and respect one another. One of my and Dr. Stead's mentors, Dr. Paul Dudley White, stated:

For...years, I have treasured the idea...that physicians of all nations...might bring together, not only colleagues in a united crusade against disease, but multitudes of patients to promote international friendship and...world peace.... The...science of peace is long overdue. It is my...hope that I have contributed in some... measure to its coming.

Pacemakers are frequently life-saving devices. They almost invariably improve the quality of life for the recipient. But, pacemakers serve a greater purpose; they foster peace and understanding between a country's inhabitants in which our pacemaker bank is established and the U. S. With each heartbeat, one can imagine the word, 'peace...peace...peace'; or is it 'paz...paz... paz?'; or is it 'paix...paix...paix?'

In an effort to "be kind to the earth" the roots for Heartbeat International were planted by Dr. Federico Alfaro of Guatemala. Dr. Alfaro was a medical resident and cardiology fellow in the Department of Medicine at Baylor College of Medicine in Houston when I was the department's chair.

After his training, Federico returned to his native Guatemala to practice cardiology and influence the health of his people. He discovered the role poverty plays making modern medical technologies inaccessible for many people.

When he became the President of the Club Rotario Guatemala de la Asuncion in 1977, he established the first pacemaker bank. He collected over 50 cardiac pacemakers, many which had been previously used. Many of these devices had several years of battery life remaining. They were sterilized and re-implanted in an approved recipient. When the pacemaker was no longer needed, usually because of the death of the individual, it was returned to the bank. Pacemakers were loaned by Dr. Alfaro's supervised bank to patients in many other Latin American countries. I learned of the program organized by Dr. Alfaro and expanded it. Such a program required the shipping of used pacemakers across international borders and was plagued by many problems-liability, FDA regulations, lack of support of manufacturers, etc.

Thus, Heartbeat International was created under my directorship in 1985 based in my home state, Florida. Leaders of Rotary International, based in Illinois, agreed to support this program, distributing new pacemakers to developing countries worldwide. Since that time, many manufacturers [i.e. Medtronic, U.S.A. Inc., St. Jude Medical, S.C. Inc., Guidant Inc., Pacesetter Inc.] have contributed over 5,000 pacemakers.

The success of this program which has created a network sites, sponsoring 43 Pacemaker Banks in 27 developing countries. All but the two banks in the People's Republic of China [Chengdu, Kunming] are supervised by local Rotary Clubs; these two are directed by university medical school committees. The program has been responsible for implantation of over 4,000 pacemakers, and donations of over one and a half million dollars in equipment. Support is provided by regional organizations, like the Rotary Clubs, the American College of Cardiology, and the North American Society of Pacing and Electrophysiology. In addition, there is ongoing cooperation from foreign governmental agencies, as well as travel grants for foreign doctors to attend meeting in this country.

Two years after Heartbeat International was established, an educational program was developed to bring a physician from each pacemaker bank around the world to an annual workshop devoted to medical education subjects. This workshop is always held in conjunction with the Annual Scientific Session of the American College of Cardiology. Such meetings are directed at improving medical knowledge in developing countries and fostering international understanding and goodwill.

In 1986, then President Reagan recognized Heartbeat International as one of 100 organizations nationwide "for outstanding service to the community and finding innovative private solutions to public problems". There are many other opportunities in the private sector for to take initiative to foster international understanding and world peace through Medicine and hasten the goal of Dr. White: "The coming of the science of peace."

Henry D. McIntosh, M.D., M.A.C.C.
Former Pres. of The Amer. College of
Cardiology
Founder, Council on Geriatric
Cardiology [jj,kk,ll]

Translation of Latin phrase: A load cheerfully borne becomes light.

Chapter References
[in order of their appearance in the above text]

a. Lown, B. The Lost Art of Healing. Ballantine Books, NY 1999.
b. Lown, B. A developing world fellowship. The Lown Forum. [in publication].
c. Starfield B. Is the US health really the best in the world? JAMA July 26, 2000.
d. World Health Organization. The WHO report 2000 health systems performance. Geneva:WHO, 2000.
e. Morrison I, Smith R. Hamster health care. BMJ 2000; 321: 1541-42.
f. Commonwealth Fund, Harris Interactive, Harvard. 2000 international health policy survey of physicians. New York: Commonwealth Fund, 2000.
g. Shindul-Rothschild J, et al. Keys to Quality Care. Amer J Nursing. 1997; 97: 35.
h. Report of the Ad Hoc Committee on Health Research Relating to Future Intervention Options. Investing in Health Research and Development (Summary) World Health Organization, Geneva, 1996.
i. Beaglehole R, Bonica R. Public Health at the Crossroads. Cambridge University Press, 1997.
j. Medical News Briefs: BMJ. 1 May 1993, p 1147.

k. Kevany J. Extreme poverty: an obligation ignored. BMJ. 1996;313:65.

l. Crossette B. U.N. World Bank and l.M.F. Join $25 Billion Drive for Africa. The New York Times, Sunday, March 17, 1996.

m. Harrison KA. The importance of the educated healthy woman in Africa. The Lancet 1997; 349: 644.

n. Weeks AD. And the band played on.... BMJ. 1997; 314:1629-30.

o. Murray CJL, Lopez AD. Global Comparative Assesements in the Health Sector. Geneva, Switzerland World Health Organization, 1994.

p. Dodu SRA. Emergence of cardiovascular disease in developing countries . Cardiology. 1988; 75:56-64.

q. Reddy KS. Can we telescope the transition? chronic disease epidemics in developing countries.
ProCOR: Commentary. HYPERLINK "mailto:procor@usa.healthnet.org "procor@usa.healthnet.org, 1997; 6 Nov.

r. Drewnowski A, Popkin BM. The nutrition transition: New trends in the global diet. Nutrition Reviews, 1997; 55 :31-34.

s. Halstead SB, Walsh JA, Warren KS. (eds): Good Health at Low Cost. Conference Report, The Rockefeller Foundation Bellagio, 1985.

t. Woolhandler S, Himmelstein DU Labar B, Lang S. Transplanted technology: third world options and first word science. NEJM. 1987; 317:504-506.

u. UNESCO Statistical Yearbook 1985. (Tables 6 and 10).

v. Bergstrom S. The pathology of poverty in: Lankinen KS. et al. see above ref 4B, p. 3-12.

x. Bukachi F. Primary health care and HealthNet; Whydah September, 1996; 5 no3. p 3-5.

y. Personal communication Jean G. Shaw Research Officer SatelLife UK report on visit to the 5th Congress The Association for Health Information and Libraries in Africa; September, 1996.

z. Rosenberg D. Can libraries in Africa ever be sustainable? Inform Develop. 1994; 10: 247-251.

aa. Personal communication: Irene Bertrand, WHO Library, Geneva. 1997.

bb. Lohr Steve. The great unplugged masses confront the future. New York Times. 21 April , 1996.

cc. Reddy KS, Yusuf S. Emerging epidemic of cardiovascular disease in developing countries. Circulation 1998; 97; 596-601.

dd. Cooper RS, Rotini CN, Kaufman JS, Muna WFT, Menash G. Hypertension treatment and control in sub-Saharan Africa: the epidemiological basis for policy. BMJ 1998; 316:614-617.

ee. Lown B. Health technology, the developing world and SatelLife. ProCOR: Commentary. <HYPERLINK "mailto: procor @usa.healthnet.org"procor@usa.healthnet.org , 1997; February.

ff. Lopez AD. Assessing the burden of mortality from cardiovascular disease. World Health Stat Q. 1993; 46: 91-96.

ff0. Omran AR. The epidemiogical transition - a theory of the epidemiology of population change. Milbank Memorial Fund Q 1971, 4: 509-38.

ff1. Tolstoy L. What Then Must We Do? 1886.

gg. Logie DE, Benatar SR. Africa in the 21st Century: Can despair be turned to hope? BMJ.1997; 315:1444-6.

hh. Lown B. Cardiology at a crossroad: challenge for India. [in publication], April 2001.

ii. Lown B, Bukachi F, Xavier R. Health information and the developing world. Lancet [suppl.], 1998. 175; 352, sII34-38.

jj. McIntosh HD. Can we afford not to reuse cardiac pacemakers? Can J Cardiol. 8; 7: 687-689.

kk. McIntosh HD, Conti CR, Vlietsra RE, Gonzales JL. Heartbeat International: A cooperative program using pacemakers to foster international goodwill and understanding. Transactions of the Amer Clin and Climatological Assoc. 1986; 98: 187-196.

ll. McIntosh HD. [personal communication]. February, 2001.

Considering Challenges with Dr. Stead

Epilogue

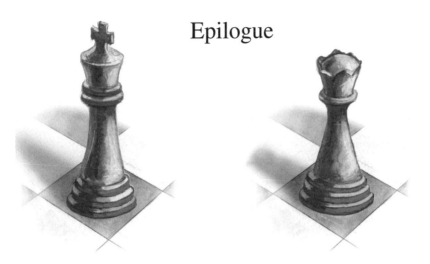

Endgame: **The Closing Bell**
[Tag, You're It]
by Robert L. Bloomfield, DUMC, '77
and Adam S. Bloomfield, Duke '04

In teaching the medical student, the primary requisite is to keep him awake. [22]   Chevalier Jackson

Looking back on Dr. Stead's illustrious career, leaves me a little speechless; something that I'm not that used to. Thank goodness there are many others I can rely on to chime in their 'two cents' when I'm at a loss for words [quite a bit less than Stead's nickel bets with housestaff regarding a clinical problem]. One constant reminder of his pervasive effects on medical practice shows up in my daily interactions with my own limited circle of practitioners and friends. We will be sitting around the dinner table and I will mention Eugene Stead and forks will suddenly freeze in mid-mouth position, with arms suspended, while each guest pauses to express how Stead affected their current careers from afar; this prolonged hiatus in the evening meal is not due to my questionable cooking techniques, though I'm infamous for my petrified 'gray casserole', my tuna salad laced with fresh grapes on a garlic bagel, and my uncanny propensity to burn Jello [How does he do *that* !!??].

To many, Dr. Eugene A. Stead, Jr. is a conundrum. He is certainly complicated, but really he is not that complicated. I have begun to think with the time allotted to me, that he is basically a blend of two contrasting characteristics represented by Nietzsche and the old slogan from Nike; "just do it!" He's a modern philosopher-king, but not quite what Plato had in mind. He's definitely more Nike than Nietzsche.

Some of his goals now seem to involve informing younger generations regarding the enjoyment of taking care of people and improving both healthcare and medical education. Dr. Tinsley Harrison, the famous cardiologist, for whom the textbook of medicine was named, suggested Dr. Stead retire from the academic realm before age 60. Harrison may have been right, but Stead just retired out of one thing and right into another. I hope he doesn't retire again out of whatever he's doing or not doing now; not likely. Harvey Cushing didn't either, even when others told him he should. Dr. Stead and I have talked about making a TV miniseries about his life; personally, I think Richard Chamberlain would be essential to the cast. He's had some medical experience playing Dr. Kildare.

It was merely by chance that I discovered that Dr. Eugene Stead was very much alive and well north of my old stomping ground, Durham, NC. Even though I don't smoke, I had the urge to extinguish my imaginary cigarette on my way to visit him and his wife, Evelyn, for my first time at their self-built home on Kerr Lake. My family was greeted with great hospitality, two large, friendly dogs, and stories of late nights on the wards, low-fat cookery, and stories of antique lamps [I haven't seen all of them yet, but I will]. We've been back several times; for barbecue, more hospitality, tours around the Stead homestead, bucolic quiet peppered with ruminations and peace.

Many years and miles have not diminished Dr. Stead's impact on the medical profession. Through his associations with others, his impact may have global repercussions and aftershocks. He always had a way of maximizing his efforts even when it concerned geological time. Still, he was wrong about one aspect of 'the forgetting curve' he coined; alas, he miscalculated the half-life of his [radioactive] effect on medicine; its decay is very slow and he will be remembered for a very long time, indeed.

Penultimate Challenge:

The path of scholarship is similar to Chickadaunce's theory on the reality of form via everything. "If you want to draw a vase you cannot draw just the vase. You have to draw the apple, bowl, cloth, wall, and the table. And you have to draw them all at the same time." The vase by itself is out of space and time. An object is only real through its relation to everything else; and that goes for people too. In short, that means that we cannot understand

229

anything or anybody until we understand everything. This, of course, is impossible currently.

Let's look at this in the context of academia (just one of several venues into scholarship). Think of facts as geometric points. They exist but lack any real dimension. Standing alone, they are not real and those who study only facts, no matter how many facts they study, are not scholars. However, to see points in context is a step in the right direction. One can learn ways of knowing. We now no longer have points, but lines that connect points; there is now a sense of cohesion in an area of knowledge. To push this idea of 'connectedness' further, the next step is to see the overlappings of different ways of knowing; see the relations between seemingly dissimilar ideas. The lines have aggregated to form shapes. Now, despite all this interweaving and overlapping, the form in question, this collective understanding, is only two-dimensional. What remains to be clarified is the relation of that 'connectedness' in the context of one's life. There is a point when you see a piece of artwork that reminds you of a story that reminds you of an event that reminds you of your mother (or something else close to home). Now one has what I call a bigger blur of truth. Thus, scholarship is not an endeavor outside or beyond one's everyday life. It is an integration of connection and identity.

So now we have gone from point to line to shape and finally to a definite form. With the integration of identity we have a bigger blur of truth that is now real and tangible. Despite all this meaning, this larger blur of truth is still a form without function. The question is: 'What good can one do with this blur of truth?' One comes to see oneself as the point, itself, in need of connection. A person armed with a big blur of truth still has very little clout standing alone. This final step answers the question "why?" about scholarship. It is this moral purpose and action, that makes the search worthwhile; worth a lifetime of searching.

The path of scholarship, is not one of glory, or power, or money. It is one of sacrifice and sometimes, even failure. Do not pursue scholarship for a site-specific destination. Pursue it because it is right. Eventually, your understanding, your fame, and even your identity, will pass on. But the moral action one took to connect with humanity, the good works that one has done, will live on for many generations to come.

adapted from a speech:
Adam Samuel, Duke University, '04

On the way back from 'Honah Lee' [the name taken from the song, *Puff the Magic Dragon*], the gated retreat on Kerr Lake where the Steads reside, I was daydreaming [actually, 'duskdreaming'] and bathing in the wisdom imparted to me after a wonderful meal provided by the Steads [it included crowder peas]. Dr. Jim Wyngaarden had joined us and he and my children and my wife and Evelyn and I argued about religion with the eldest statesman; I think Dr. Stead won that round. The current Chairman of Medicine at Wake Forest University Medical Center, Dr. Applegate, tried to argue with him at a geriatric meeting once; he lost too. You just can't win easily with Eugene Stead.

Now, when I lecture to my children, they invariably roll back their eyes and chime in anticipation, "Oh no, dad's gonna quote Dr. Stead again." No, Stead's not always right; but, it is hard to argue with many things he has said. [There, that'll shut them younguns of mine up for a while. Now, I can go back to my duskdreaming as we get on the highway toward home.]

Stead's great stature is, in part, due to his willingness to give credit to a lot of other people who carried on a medical tradition and passed a torch; people like Lown, McIntosh, Hickam, Wyngaarden, Kerby, and you know who [yes, especially, Kempner, too]. So many people added little pieces to a perpetual puzzle that kept changing shape and filled in the area beneath or above the 'forgetting curve.' [Oh!, for joy!, I just knew my premed years of calculus would come in handy in deriving a post-medical school life function, one of these days.]

As these great physicians have matured, they have become more brilliant; more enlightened; more willing to share their knowledge with others, especially those less fortunate. In addition, they've utilized more of their abilities to generate resources to improve the healthcare system. Stead, in particular, has taught others a way of thinking that can be applied to any worthy endeavor. He taught many colleagues to never stop being child-like scholars in their pursuit of Medicine; *and* to never stop *frolicking in the autumn mist in a land called Honah Lee;* as Peter, Paul, and Mary kept repeating.

I'm sure we'll see Dr. Eugene Stead and perhaps, some other 'greats' several times again; and each time we've gone to Kerr Lake, there's always somebody else around visiting that couple. If you should be fortunate enough to see Dr. and Mrs. Stead at their place at the lake and stay past sunset, and you find yourself duskdreaming: Wake up!!, for heaven's sake; remember something amidst your reverie; would you please turn out the lights when you leave??!! [Careful, don't bump your head as you go out the door. Later, ya hear?!]

Latin Quotes translated in order of their appearance [also noted at the end of each section]:

Preface-"an unorthodox sage of rough genius"

Introduction-"realize how much you have still to learn"

Chapter 1- "I am Davus, not Oedipus." "I am an ordinary man, no solver of riddles like Oedipus."

Chapter 2- "by disuse are privileges lost."

Chapter 3- "judge a tree by it's fruit not it's leaves."

Chapter 4- "a devourer of books"

Chapter 5- "work itself is pleasure"

Chapter 6- "the doctor treats, nature cures"; prior to poem, "scholarship without morals is useless"

Chapter 7- "repetition is the mother of studies"

Chapter 8- "for how many evils is religion responsible"

Chapter 9- "experience will teach you many things"

Chapter 10-"light (comes) out of the East, law from the West."

Chapter 11-"a load cheerfully borne becomes light."

Considering Challenges with Dr. Stead

Afterword and Afterthought

by Eugene A. Stead, M.D.

edited by Robert L. Bloomfield, M.D., DUMC '77 and Brandon L. Craven, premed student, Duke '04, final editing by Adam S. Bloomfield, Duke '04

Below we have summarized recent correspondence to colleagues written by Dr. Stead. He calls this his "last hurrah" at his full 92 and one half years. We think of it, however, as 'more of the same' [or at least, similar]; a frank and creative continuation of a way of thinking that started so many years ago near Atlanta. We hope that this form of cognition is cautiously carried on for many generations to come by many of Stead's studious descendants.

Most economists believe that absolute monopolies are undesirable and our laws allow them to be broken up. Many of us remember the legal actions leading to the breakup of the Rockefeller oil empire, the tobacco trust of James B. Duke, and more recently, the troubles surrounding Microsoft. One group of civilian institutions has established a monopoly which can only be broken up by repealing laws in all the states. All fifty states require applicants who wish to be given the privilege of practicing medicine to pass state approved qualifying examinations. At first glance this may seem quite reasonable; no one wants to be under the care of an unqualified physician. The catch is that no American citizen can sit for the qualifying examinations until he or she has graduated from an accredited medical school. The monopoly cannot be broken nationally without changes in the laws of all states. The monopoly drives up the cost of medical care, and it is this monopoly that is partly to blame for the present state of our health care system.

Many agencies are currently studying problems present in our health care system; these agencies are dominated by faculty members of our top medical schools. It is in their interest to allow the monopoly to continue. The leaders of the monopoly sleep well. They have never been challenged. After all, they are the ones with the power, the time, and the financial resources to produce change.

Interestingly, any accredited medical school has the power to break this monopoly. Once a medical school is accredited, it has the privilege of filling its classes with students who have graduated from a four-year college. It can accept students for advanced standing and award the MD degree whenever the school believes that the student is ready for the qualifying exams. About 35 years ago, an experiment by a Florida medical school made up for a collapse in the market for Ph.D. graduates by allowing certain Ph.D. candidates to enter directly into the third year of medical school. In my role as physician-in-chief of Duke hospital, I appointed several of these Ph.D. candidates to the resident staff. They performed as well as, and in some instances, better than students who had spent four years in medical school. The traditional path to medicine, four years of college instruction followed by four years of medical school, is not always necessary to prepare quality students.

In fairness to medical schools, all of the allied health disciplines have developed in parallel as vertical spikes and they have usually made no provision to allow horizontal movement from one profession to another. If one desires to broaden his base and climb another spike, he must start at the bottom of the new spike, with no credit given for any past-related learning.

Accepting the fact that our attempts to break the medical monopoly have failed, we offer a way around it that should leave the monopoly intact. To understand our proposal, you will need to know more about medical schools and their educational programs.

Medical schools traditionally require 4 years of course work in an accredited college. Most parents do not know that medical schools traditionally accept students from a relatively few colleges. The colleges sending the most students to medical schools are allied to the medical school monopoly. Many schools cannot survive without the tuition paid by third and fourth year premedical students, so they use their ties with the powerful medical schools to ensure that four years of college education is required, and that the colleges will continue to receive the students' tuition money. Similarly, medical schools want support from tuition of first and second year pre-clinical students, so they require that medical school be four years long. This reluctance to budge on entrance requirements serves to increase the cost of receiving a medical education. By now we would have already made moves to break up the monopoly, if it was not protected by state laws.

The tie between favored colleges and medical schools was emphasized to me years ago by Goodrich White, the president of Emory University. I, his 33 year old professor of medicine and department chair, had told a reporter of the Atlanta Constitution that the medical school did not need to require four years of college work, two years were adequate. This would allow the students to graduate two years earlier and give them time for two additional years of postgraduate study either here or abroad. I gave my talk on Saturday night and it was headlined in the Sunday morning paper. I was surprised to receive a six thirty a.m. call from President White. "Young man! Meet me in my office at seven o'clock!" He sat me in a chair and told me that I would be fired if I ever again suggested that the medical students did not need four years of undergraduate education. "Seventy five percent of the students enrolled in classes come here because it is well known that medical schools favor Emory graduates. Emory cannot survive if we lose the money paid by third and fourth year premedical students."

Medical schools typically divide the four years of required work into two sections; pre-clinical and clinical, each are two academic years in length. The work in the pre-clinical years is designed to give students a working knowledge of the current state of the biological sciences that relate to curative and preventive medicine. A student spends two years memorizing scientific facts to ensure that he or she can pass the state qualifying examination given at the end of two years.

Putting the name 'medical' on anything increases the cost. Many excellent colleges have strong science faculties who enjoy

237

students and prize the opportunity to watch them grow. Mount Holyoke College comes to mind. This college could prepare its undergraduate science majors to take the first qualifying examination required by the states. Those going the traditional route of four years of college could, instead, remain at Mount Holyoke for an additional two years and receive a master's degree in the sciences related to clinical medicine. If the medical monopoly were broken, Mount Holyoke graduates could enter medical schools as third year students at an amazing savings of time and money.

In October 1941, I was 32 years of age and a member of the faculty of the Harvard Medical School with the rank of Associate. I was a captain of the newly formed Brigham Hospital Unit headed by Eliot Cutler; surgeon-in-chief of the Brigham Hospital. He told us to prepare for a long war. At that time, I was asked to come to Emory as Professor of Medicine and Chairman of the Department. I was to be in Atlanta by May 1944. With no help from me, Emory managed my discharge from that unit. I accepted the Emory offer but, I would not and did not make any move to avoid service.

All of my Harvard friends thought I had lost my mind. Emory and Grady Hospital had destroyed the academic careers of a series of other young men. "You have a bright future at Harvard, stay put!!" My chief, Soma Weiss, however, thought differently-"You can stay comfortably at Harvard and probably in time attain the rank of Professor. Can one person greatly influence a unit the size of Harvard-rarely. I rank you as a man of great promise; Emory needs you and if you can crack that wilderness you will have become a man of achievement. If you fail, Atlanta will have an excellent practicing physician. Go for it!" So I did. I left Harvard to accept a position at Emory.

With the war underway, the number of interns and residents assigned to a given hospital was sharply reduced. The number assigned to Grady Hospital could not cover the services. I would be telling students how to take care of patients correctly; they would find that the theory and my actual practice were quite separate. At rounds each morning, the interns, medical students, residents, nurses, and I worked with patients to find out what they wanted. We then worked to determine whether our group could meet the needs of the patient. We had the knowledge and skills to give immediate care to the most pressing problems, but regarding

238

longer-term management of patients over time, many questions arose for which our group had no answers. Each member, including myself, was assigned a question to be answered at rounds the next day. The system worked; the group knew that around midnight they could find me in the library searching for the answer to my question. In 'normal' times, it took four years in college and four years in medical school to obtain the MD degree. During the war, the college requirement was cut to two years; time in medical school to merely 27 months.

The answer to my problem of how to give excellent medical care to the sick patients on my medical wards was simple. I explained to students that their student days were over. From now on they would act as doctors. They would sleep in resident quarters and be on call day and night. Anyone had the privilege of refusing this promotion and remaining a student. In a short time, the armed services would order my reluctant students to active duty. The other students rose to meet the challenges placed before them, as will capable students today.

The student doctors saw the patients first and recorded the patient's story and findings Within the next few hours a resident or faculty member met with the patient and the student doctor to review the record and check findings. At times, the student doctor stood his ground and the record reflected his disagreement. That student invariably earned an A+ when I learned of this. I was amazed at how quickly student doctors became real doctors.

Accepting the fact that the public does not know that no significant changes in medical care will occur until the medical monopoly is broken, and that our political leaders are unaware of or apathetic to the medical school monopoly, I have outlined a program that would allow a single medical school to bypass this monopoly. The medical school that implements this program will be the first truly international medical school. It will have students from every country and will be remembered as the leader that made medical care available at a reasonable price worldwide.

An accredited medical school will establish an online division that allows students to take courses at home or at work. The purpose of the online division is to allow Physician Assistants and Nurse Practitioners holding a masters degree to take the courses needed to meet the requirements of the medical school for the MD degree. Those upgraded students would sit for the qualifying examinations alongside graduates of the traditional medical school. This would allow an easy comparison of the two methods of education. Past experience shows that older students, knowing why they are in school and anxious to make up for lost time, perform better than the younger ones. The online medical school would set the admission requirements. The final requirement would assure that the candidate has completed three years of practice under the supervision of a practicing MD or a group of MDs willing to write strong supporting letters.

I know from experience that the nursing hierarchy will resent the upgrading of nurses into MD provinces, but I cannot think of another way. Once the nurse practitioner has the MD degree, she is free. I know of no other way for the nurse to be able to take advanced training in the medical and surgical specialties. If nurses cannot crack the present glass ceiling under which the profession operates, their profession will continue to experience a declining pool of applicants to nursing schools.

To date, I have found no medical school that is willing to offer online courses. Indeed, the one thing that members of the monopoly fear is that some small school may break ranks and cause the entire edifice to crumble. Small schools are reluctant to move; they've already had a hard enough time becoming accredited.

There have been many studies that have shown that Physician Assistants operating as a part of the physician team give services equal to that of the supervising doctors. The present proposal is unacceptable to medical schools because it would undermine their legalized monopoly. I hope that the first medical school to implement this program will remember that the goal of this program is to increase the number of practicing doctors in rural and under-served areas. I would start the online program with a few students that would spend a short time on the medical school campus in the summer before they matriculated. The online dean, with the help of the traditional medical school faculty, would determine what additional courses each student needed to be able to pass the qualifying examinations. These students could take both of the qualifying examinations in the same week. The three years of practice during which the online students cared for patients everyday would give our online students sitting for the exams clinical skills and knowledge far beyond that possessed by those graduating from the usual on-campus medical school.

Taking the traditional route through medical school is expensive and time consuming. If this route could be shortened through less time either in college or in medical school or by allowing members of other health careers to receive credit for their experience, there would be a huge cost and time savings. This proposal would also provide one way to return medicine to the service profession it once was.

Eugene A Stead, Jr. MD
Distinguished Professor of Medicine Emeritus, Duke University Medical School, Charter Member of the Institute of Medicine, Creator of the Physician Assistants-Associates Programs

abridged and adapted from a poem: ***The Scholar-Gipsy***
                    by Matthew Arnold [1822-88]   [27]

Near me on the grass lies this book
Come, let me read the tale again!
The story of the Oxford* scholar poor,
Of quick inventive brain,
Who, tired of knocking at preferment's door,
One morn forsook some friends
and went to learn the gipsy-lore,
And roamed with that brotherhood,
And came to good, but came to Oxford no more.

*editor's note-the predecessor of Emory University, Dr. Stead's alma mater and locale of his first official chairmanship, was called, Emory at Oxford until 1952 when it was renamed Oxford College. As J. Willis Hurst, M.D., states in his book, The Quest for Excellence: "...there was once a group of scholars [here] who walked between the buildings...reading bits of classic literature...."

                                                    [23]

Years after, in the country-lanes,
Two scholars, whom at college he knew,
Met him, and of his way of life inquired;
Where at he answered, that the gipsy-crew,
Had arts to rule as they desired,
The workings of men's brains,
And they can bind them to what thoughts they will.
"And I," he said, "the secret of their art,
When fully learned, will to the world impart;
But it needs heaven-sent moments for this skill."

He left them, and returned no more.
But rumors hung about the country-side,
That the scholar long was seen to stray,
Seen by glimpses, pensive and tongue-tied,
In cloak of gray, (The same the gipsies wore).
Shepherds had met him on the hurst in spring;
At some alehouse found him at their entering.

The story ran through Oxford halls,
Many did the tale inscribe,
That thou wert wandered from the studious walls
To learn strange arts, and join a gipsy-tribe;

To the Genius, we remit our life,
But thou possessest an immortal lot,
And we imagine thee exempt from age,
And living as thou liv'st on a book's page,
Because thou hadst-what we have not.

For early didst thou leave with powers fresh,
undiverted to the world without,
Firm to their mark, not spent on other things;
Free from the sick fatigue, the languid doubt.
O life unlike ours! Who fluctuate idly without term or scope,
Of whom each strives, nor knows for what he strives,
And each half lives a hundred different lives;
Who wait like thee, but not, like thee, in hope.

We who hesitate and falter life away,
And lose tomorrow the ground won today.
Amongst us one, his seat upon the intellectual throne;
And all his store of experience lays bare,
Tells us his birth and growth and signs,
And how the dying spark of hope was fed,
And how the breast was soothed, and how the head,
    and all his hourly varied anodynes.
O born in days when wits were fresh and, life ran gaily;
Before this strange disease of modern life,
With it's sick hurry, it's divided aims, it's head
    o'ertaxed, it's palsied hearts.

Thou through the fields and through the woods dost stray,
Roaming the countryside, a truant boy,
Nursing thy projects in unclouded joy,
Every doubt long blown by time away.

From: ***The Juggler***   by Richard Wilbur, [final 2 verses] [27]

Oh, on his toe the table is turning, the broom's
Balancing up on his nose, and the plate whirls
On the tip of the broom! Damn, what a show, we cry:
The boys stamp, and the girls
Shriek, and the drum booms
And all comes down, and he bows and says good-bye.

If the juggler is tired now, if the broom stands
In the dust again, if the table starts to drop
Through the dark again, and though the plate
Lies flat on the table top,
For him we batter our hands
Who has won for once over the world's weight.

References

1. Hurst, JW., Eugene Auston Stead, Jr., MD: A conversation with J. Willis Hurst, MD *The Amer. Jl. of Card.* 1999.; 84; 701-725.

2. Warren, James, V., and Stead, Eugene, A. ,Jr. Fluid dynamics in chronic congestive heart failure. *Arch. of Intern. Med.* 1944; 73. 138-147.

3. Warren, James V. J. Eugene A. Stead, Jr. *Clin Cardiol.* 1986.; 9; 233-235.

4. Beeson, Paul, B. Eugene A. Stead, Jr.: A biographical note. *Ann. of Intern. Med.* 1968.; 69; 986-989.

5. Stead, Eugene, A., Jr. Walter Kempner: A perspective. *Arch. Intern. Med.* 1974.; 133; 756-757.

6. McIntosh, Henry, D. The Eugene A. Stead, Jr., Symposium [introduction]. *Ann. of Intern. Med.* 1968.; 69; 993-995.

7. DeBakey, Michael, E. [letter to author]. Baylor College of Medicine, Houston. April 24, 2000.

8. McIntosh, HD, Morris, JJ, Whalen, RE, et. al. Bilateral functional subaortic stenosis in the alligator. *Amer. Clinical and Climatolological Assn.* 1967.; 78; 119-128.

9. McIntosh, HD and Garcia, JA. The first decade of aorto-coronary bypass grafting, 1967-1977. *Circ.* 1978.; 57; 405-431.

10. Ross, Joseph, C., [Editorial], John Bamber Hickam. *Arch. of Intern. Med. 1971;* 127; 569-570.

11. Ross, Joseph, C. Hickam Symposium [introduction]. *Arch. of Intern. Med.* 1971; 127; 571-573.

12. Saylor, Galen. The World Book Multimedia Encyclopedia. Chicago, IL. c. 1999.

13. Stead, Eugene A., Jr, The evolution of the medical university. *Jl. of Med. Ed.*; 39; April, 1964. 368-373.

14. Stead, Eugene. A., Jr, Physicians-past and future. *Arch. of Intern. Med* .127; 703-707.

15. DeBakey, Lois. [letter to author]. Baylor College of Medicine, Houston. July, 2000.

16. Haynes, Barton. <u>A Way of Thinking:</u> *A Primer on the Art of Being a Doctor.* Carolina Academic Press. Durham, NC. c. 1989; 33-39.

17. Stead, Eugene, A., Jr, Medical Intelligence. Training and use of paramedical personnel. *NEJM.* Oct. 12, 1967; 800-801.

18. Stead, Eugene, A., Jr, Medical care: It's social and organizational aspects. *.NEJM.* 1963; 269;240-244.

19. Stead, Eugene, A., Jr, Medical education and practice. *Ann. of Intern. Med.* 1979; 72; 271-274.

20. Stead, Eugene, A., Jr, Why moon walking is simpler than social progress. [Editorial]. *Medical Times.* November, 1969.

21. Chandler, TE and Bloomfield, RL. <u>The Foremost Physician, The Farseeing Physician.</u> Harbinger Medical Press, NC. c.1983.; 1-105.

22. Bloomfield, RL. <u>One Q.D. Calender.</u> c.1985. Harbinger Medical Press, Winston-Salem, NC.

23. Hurst, J. W. <u>The Quest for Excellence: The history of the Department of Medicine at Emory University School of Medicine 1834-1986.</u> Atlanta: Scholars Press. 1997.;1-583.

24. Osler, William. <u>Aequanimitas with other Addresses.</u> 1932.; 3; 1-451.

25.Bloomfield, RL and Chandler, ET. <u>Mnemonics Rhetoric and Poetics for Medics.</u> Harbinger Medical Press, NC. c.1982.; vol. 1; 1-222.

26. Wagner, GS, Cebe, B, Rozear, MP. <u>Stead, Eugene, A. Jr.: What this patient needs is a doctor.</u> Carolina Academic Press. Durham, NC. c. 1981.; 1-244.

27. Harmon, William [ed.]. <u>The Top 500 Poems.</u> Columbia University Press, New York. c.1992.; 1-1132.

28. Lazslo, John. The Doctor's Doctor [unpublished manuscript], Atlanta, c. 1975.1-535.

29. Stead, EA and Weiss, SH?. Effect of paredrinol on sodium nitrate collapse and on clinical shock. *J. Clin. Invest.* 18: 679, 1939.

30. Stead, EA and Ebert, RH. Shock syndrome produced by failure of the heart. *Arch. Int. Med.* 69: 369, 1942.

31. Stead, EA and Warren, JV. Orientation to the mechanisms of clinical shock. *Arch. Surg.* 50:1, 1945.

32. Stead, EA and Warren, JV. Cardiac output in man. An analysis of the mechanisms varying the cardiac outpatient based on recent clinical studies. *Arch. Int. Med.* 80: 237, 1947.

33. Stead, EA. The role of cardiac output in the mechanisms of congestive heart failure. *Am. J. Med.* 6: 232, 1949.

34. Lown, B. <u>Practicing the Art while Mastering the Science,</u> c.2000. Harbinger Medical Press, Winston-Salem, NC. 59-62.

Soon Available from
Harbinger Medical Press:

Teacher and Student
*a CD with original musical compositions
and excerpts from Sir William Osler
[includes lyrics to parody sung to theme from "The Beverly
Hillbillies"-'Let me tell you a story 'bout a man named Stead']*

Call or fax 336 7689827 or send this page
to Harbinger Medical Press, P.O. Box 17201,
Winston-Salem, NC 27116

To order this or any other item listed in the front of this book, call
or write Harbinger Medical Press as noted above.

248